MW01265048

THE STRONG HAND OF THE LORD

Its Blessing, Power and Fury

By Malcolm W. (Chip) Hill, Jr.

The Strong Hand of the Lord, by Malcolm W. (Chip) Hill, Jr.
ISBN # 0-89228-154-5
Copyright 2005, Malcolm W. Hill, Jr.

Published by
Impact Christian Books, Inc.
332 Leffingwell Ave.,
Kirkwood, MO 63122
www.impactchristianbooks.com

Cover Design: *Ideations*

Printed in the United States of America

Table of Contents

Preface

THANK YOU . . .

I would like to thank Chris Patrick for his computer "know how" which is invaluable, as well as his generosity in sharing his library of study helps.

I would also like to thank Katie Patrick – my aide-de-camp – whose enthusiasm and early editing work were crucial.

Also, I want to thank Rhonda White, whose last minute editing work helped to catch anything Bill Banks, Katie or I might have missed

Finally, thanks **Word of Faith** and **Faith Covenant**. Your support in every way is essential to my ministry as an author of Christian books. I love you all. You are both such wonderful church families.

Table of Contents

Preface

THANK YOU . . .

I would like to thank Chris Patrick for his computer "know how" which is invaluable, as well as his generosity in sharing his library of study helps.

I would also like to thank Katie Patrick – my aide-de-camp – whose enthusiasm and early editing work were crucial.

Also, I want to thank Rhonda White, whose last minute editing work helped to catch anything Bill Banks, Katie or I might have missed

Finally, thanks **Word of Faith** and **Faith Covenant**. Your support in every way is essential to my ministry as an author of Christian books. I love you all. You are both such wonderful church families.

Preface

In recent years a needed emphasis has been placed on seeking the face of the Lord rather than His hand and what it can provide. In fact, the words of a popular worship song say, "We do not seek Your hand, we only seek Your face." These words offer some correction to a generation of Christians that has put more emphasis on satisfying its own desires through prayer, rather than the desire God has for intimate fellowship with His people. The Bible even records a wondrous dialogue between God and the sweet Psalmist of Israel. David prayed, "When You said, 'Seek My face,' my heart said to You, 'Your face, Lord, I will seek'" (27:8). A beautiful picture of devotion cries to us from this verse, inspiring us to draw close to the Lord in enjoyable communion. I believe many in our generation are hearing this cry, and they have begun to respond by declaring, "Lord, I want to love You for who You are, and not simply for what You do!" This has always been the greater reason for communion with God. However, if we are not careful, such a desire may remove from us the *legitimate* pursuit of the Lord's hand, which empties out blessings on our lives. Indeed, nothing is wrong with seeking the hand of the Lord *if* we are also seeking His face. Nothing is wrong with seeking His hand *if* we truly fear Him. Indeed, we will never really know the hand of God without knowing the fear of God. But when we know both His face and His fear, there is no limit to what His hand can do for us as we seek to establish His kingdom throughout the earth.

Beloved, a manifestation of the strong hand of the Lord is coming at a time when the Church desperately needs it. It is coming at a time when God's people need supernatural help reaching the world for Christ. If all we have to give men are eloquent speeches, which showcase our intelligence but miss their hearts, we will lose the harvest God wants to give. But if we go to the nations in humility, and with an undeniable display of God's power to save, heal and deliver, multiplied millions of people will turn to the Lord and be added to the Church. So come, let us learn about the hand of our God, and with great resolve impact the nations.

1

I Will Teach You
About the Hand of God

This chapter title comes from the ancient book of Job. Amidst his season of intense suffering, Job made this statement to the friends who came to comfort him.

I will teach you about the hand of God; what is with the Almighty I will not conceal. Surely all of you have seen it; why then do you behave with complete nonsense?

Job 27:11-12

With an imperfect knowledge based on what he had seen, heard or experienced in life, Job attempted to teach his friends some things about the hand of the Lord. It is certain that although his knowledge was limited, he was willing to tell them all he knew.

With God's invisible attributes clearly seen in nature, no one really has an excuse for disregarding Him. (See Psalm 19:1-4; Romans 1:20.) Job had seen His power in the world around him; his friends had seen it too, so none of them were justified in approaching life in a thoughtless and careless manner. And so it is with you and me. Whether we have seen the Lord in a beautiful sunset, a raging storm, a mountainside aglow with fall foliage, or in the pages of His sacred Book, none of us can claim ignorance and thus ignore the universal call to worship and serve our Creator. And yet as we look across the world, we see a vast host of people who are completely out-of-touch with the reality and power of the Lord. They may know the power of money, of science, of political persuasion or military might, but unless they know God's face *and* His hand, they are handicapped when facing the stark realities of a hostile spiritual world.

The Hand

Let us consider more closely those peculiar appendages attached at the end of our arms—the hands. They consist of a larger part with two sides—the palm and the back of the hand—as well as bony knuckles situated at the base of five long digits called fingers, one of which is a thumb. Although they are a relatively small part of the human body, they are a most significant part. Imagine life without your hands. You wouldn't be able to pick up things, you wouldn't be able to defend yourself, and you would be hard-pressed to ply a trade or talent.

When your own hand comes upon something, it usually does so in order to cause the thing to do what it is unable to do itself. A fork lies dormant on the table until your hand puts it to good use. Your hand can grip a hammer, twist a screwdriver, or take up a weapon, manipulating what otherwise would be inactive if your hand had not seized it. Your hand can pet an animal, turn a doorknob, or squeeze paste on a toothbrush. It can be the means by which you bless and comfort others, or bring them great harm. With the hand you can dole out blessings or withhold them. Your hand can be a caressing tool of comfort, or a damaging fist of fury and wrath. It can scratch, squeeze, pull along or shove away, serving as a tool for God's glory or an implement of destruction that satisfies no one but the Devil and his demons. Amidst trials and temptation you can either lift up your hands in praise, or allow them to hang down in defeat (Hebrews 12:12). Any way we look at it, our hands are important—even essential tools for life and service. God's hands are no different. He can stretch out His hands to heal, like He did the leper in Mark 1:41, or He can use them to bring judgment on the heads of His enemies, as when He blinded an evil sorcerer on Cyprus (Acts 13:11). He can use His hand to add great numbers of souls to the Church as in Antioch (Acts 11:21), or He can take up the winnowing fan and thoroughly purge His threshing floor of human chaff (Matthew 3:12).

One of the greatest things God's hand does today is come upon helpless human beings like you and me. When His mighty hand lays hold of the willing soul, the blessing He can release is enormous. Like a fork lying motionless on a table, our lives don't amount for much without the influence of His Spirit. That is why it is so important for each of us to yield to the Holy Spirit as we seek to make our lives count for eternity. It was Micah the prophet who said, "But I am truly full of power, by the Spirit of the Lord" (3:8). Let this be both our individual and corporate testimony.

Spirit and Power: Synonyms for His Hand

When we speak of God's hand, we refer to His Spirit and His power. In many cases the Word simply says, "And the Spirit of the Lord came mightily upon him," or "the power of the Lord came upon him." Therefore, we see that God's hand, His power, and His Spirit are pretty much the same thing. When His hand comes upon a person, extraordinary things begin to happen.

When God's hand came upon Samson, he was able to tear apart a fierce young lion, carry the gates of a city on his back, and bludgeon a thousand Philistines with the jawbone of an ass. These amazing exploits were accomplished as the hand of the Lord came upon him.

Nowadays God's hand doesn't usually affect us for such physical feats as these, although it does sometimes happen. (Don't credit adrenalin with every mighty action taken.) However, God's Spirit does endue us "with power from on high," so that we might effectively preach the gospel and extend the kingdom in this Church age (Luke 24:49).

When an apostle travels the globe every year, preaching to multitudes, surviving on food that would kill a goat, and thriving on less than four hours sleep a night, somebody's hand must be on him. With an apostolic call comes an apostolic grace. I call this grace the hand of the Lord.

When an evangelist is able to stand up in a crowded airport terminal and preach to more than a hundred restless travelers who await permission to board their flight—and not be shouted down, but win them all to the Lord—that's the hand of God on his life. (The late Bob Shattles did this on several occasions.)

When a local pastor is able to endure all kinds of pressure from inside and outside the church, and not burn out or cave in, but keep his joy and sense of mission, the hand of the Lord is on his life.

When a believer is able to hold down a regular job, and also faithfully execute his responsibilities in the local church, the hand of the Lord is upon him.

Life without the hand of the Lord would be insipid and laborious, like a drink of dirty, soapy water on a boiling hot day. An existence without God's hand would be just that— an existence; drudgery as you slog through each day, and fullness of uncertainty as you approach your final years. Life without His wonderful hand would be a long walk through a desolate bog. I cannot imagine living a day without the power of God in my life.

God's Hand is Priceless

God's power is invaluable. It cannot be bested by evil or depleted by time and wear. It cannot be bought with money or sold for any earthly sum (Acts 8:18-20). It can, however, be purchased with faith and absolute devotion to Christ (Isaiah 55:1). The more one gives himself to Jesus, the more power Jesus releases to him. The more thought and study one gives to the Word he hears, the more power and virtue comes back to him (Luke 8:18, TAB). The more one pours out himself in earnest prayer and surrender, the more God pours Himself into that one's innermost being. This is a wonderful transaction! If we empty ourselves of our own self-seeking agendas, God will fill us with His Heaven-backed agenda. If we rid ourselves of our own attitudes of resentment and strife, the more love and power from God will come our way.

Friend, if you are a student of the Word, this volume will nourish your vision as well as enhance your faith. If after reading this book you do not long to see God's mighty hand moving in your life and ministry, then you are either dead spiritually or I have failed in my assignment to stir you up. A mighty end time harvest awaits us. Only through strong preaching, powerful signs, and stunning miracles, will this harvest be gathered. We therefore *must* have the hand of God on our lives for the challenges that lie ahead. When His strong hand comes upon us, we are enabled to do what otherwise we could not do.

2
The Prayer of Jabez

In recent years, Bruce Wilkinson's little book, *The Prayer of Jabez,* has stirred a lot of interest among Christians and secularists alike. We have seen this title on bookshelves in all kinds of stores, and in many different catalogues. It is an excellent tool for encouraging one's personal prayer life, and can do nothing but offer help to those who read it. Jabez' powerful prayer reads:

Oh, that You would bless me indeed, and enlarge my territory, that Your hand would be with me, and that You would keep me from evil, that I may not cause pain!
1 Chronicles 4:10

Of the five requests Jabez made in his prayer, the third request—the one about God's hand—intrigues me the most. Thousands, who now pray for the same thing, are clueless as to what they are asking. Simply voicing this prayer will not release the full blessing and power of the Lord on our lives. Other crucial ingredients must be added if we will experience all that this prayer entreats.

Faith in the God who hears and answers prayer is essential. This faith must be a living faith that rests strongly on all the Word of God says about the Lord and His promises.

Faith must also be of "the childlike brand." If one must intellectually understand all the workings of faith and God's power to answer before he can believe, he will receive little or nothing from the hand of the Lord.

Faith also works by love (Galatians 6:5). If one's heart is filled with the opposites of love (bitterness, resentment, competition and anger), then faith's effectiveness will be nullified, and God's hand will be shortened.

13

Obedience to a given command is also essential if we will see God respond to the prayer of Jabez. One cannot persist in conscious disobedience and expect God to crown his life with blessing, victory and success.

A holy lifestyle must also be in place. This requires that two rudimentary conditions first be met: One is that the petitioner be in right standing with God. This speaks of a righteousness that is not based on one's own good works, but rather on the righteousness of God in Christ. The second condition is this: That one's conduct is in keeping with the right standing he professes to have in Christ. A lifestyle that is less than this reflects a shallow religion and a glaring hypocrisy.

Another vital ingredient necessary for accessing the blessings of Jabez' prayer, and particularly the Lord's strong hand, is a firm knowledge of God's will concerning many matters in life. When we know God's will, it is much easier to utilize faith in seeing His will come to pass.

We Can Know His Will

The power of the Lord in one's life has everything to do with his knowledge of God's will, much of which is clearly revealed in the written Word. Therefore, if you are always questioning whether or not the Lord wants to act on your behalf, it is because you haven't taken the time to establish His Word in your heart. When you *know* God's will on a certain subject, you will not question whether or not He wants to act when you pray. The prayer of faith (Mark 11:24; 1 John 5:14-15) is based on the firm knowledge of God's revealed will.

The prayer of consecration and dedication, on the other hand, or, the "if-it-be-thy-will" type of prayer, is more for the person who is seeking to determine God's will concerning some particular matter. Usually this person needs to know what course of action to take, such as, where to go, what to do, when to do it, and who to do it with. For example: "Lord, *if* it be Your will for me to go to Tibet with Mike, please let me know for sure." Or, "Lord, if I am to marry Margaret, please confirm it for both of us." These answers often cannot be found in the Word of God, and so the one praying must bootlace his prayer with the phrase, "if it be Your will." However, if the prayer involves a biblical subject where there is clarity concerning God's redemptive will, he should approach the thing with boldness and confidence. For instance, if a sick man stands before me seeking healing, I will boldly base my prayer on my understanding that Jesus purchased healing for Him at the cross. I will also base my prayer on the knowledge that God has commissioned the Church to minister healing to the diseased. If the Lord has a reason for not releasing His healing power on the individual, I expect Him to tell me why, or simply tell me not to pray. But until then, I will approach the man's healing without question and without pause. Can you see the difference? The man whose heart is fixed and established in scriptural truth is a man who already knows God's will in most of life's matters. Such a person is not prone to double-mindedness or confusion when praying. Such a person often finds that God's power is readily available to handle the crisis before him. Truly, knowing God's will in most cases is synonymous with knowing His power.

Jesus explained it this way: "You do err, not knowing the Scriptures, nor the power of God" (Matthew 22:29, KJV). Knowing the Scriptures enables us to *know* God's will and know His power in our lives. One cannot truly know the latter without knowing the former. Furthermore, the "knowing" about which Jesus speaks is much more than a sophisticated intellectual knowledge, or "head" knowledge, but it denotes the subsurface *heart* knowledge that enables one to stand firm in the face of every contradiction. Such knowledge is deeply rooted in the inner man—in the hidden man of the heart—and not in one's intellectual abilities. That is why mere children can sometimes experience miracles, while highly educated psychologists and theologians can't experience anything!

When the Logos Becomes Rhema

The free and abundant release of Yahweh's power requires that certain verses and truths found in the *logos* Word, or "broad and general" Word of God, become *rhema,* or "quickened truths" to those who read and hear them. The quickened Word always produces living results! That is why Jesus said, "And you shall *know* the truth, and the truth will make you free" (John 8:32). Truly *knowing* the truth demands that something out of the *logos* become a *quickened* word to our hearts. Indeed, as we move into a deep-level knowledge of redemptive truth—knowledge of heart and not just of mind—the life of that truth will manifest powerfully in our lives! Let me give you an example.

The frightening symptoms of cancer seized me one summer, plaguing my heart and mind with fear for several weeks. It wasn't until the Spirit of God lifted Matthew 18:19 out of the *logos* and made it *rhema,* that I sensed true faith rising in my heart.

If two of you shall agree on earth as touching anything that they shall ask, it shall be done for them of my Father, which is in Heaven.

I was listening to a tape on prayer when the word "anything" in that verse was quickened to me. By the Spirit of God I was suddenly able to see that the symptoms and their cause could be categorized under the word "anything," and that if my wife, Darlene, and I could agree in faith, my healing would be manifest. This rhema may not mean much to you, but to a man in a fight, a word like this becomes a fresh jawbone with well-set teeth!

"These symptoms and their cause" I declared, "are things that are covered by the word 'anything,' and Darlene and I agree that my healing is accomplished by our Father in Heaven! Jesus said, 'If two of you agree *on earth* as touching *anything,* it shall be done for them!' Standing here on earth, we agree in both our request, and in the reception of the blessing claimed. Amen."

Fear was suddenly gone, and the divinely imparted grace of the heart called faith shone bright. For the next forty-eight hours I used this revelation in combat against fear. Within two days all symptoms of the disease were gone!

When the Philistine horde descended on Samson, shouting their threats and exclaiming what they were going to do to him, the Holy Ghost came upon him, enabling him to break the religious ropes of capitulation and compromise that bound his hands. That initial burst of Spirit power got him started in the outworking of his deliverance, but it wasn't until Samson deliberately looked around, found a fresh jawbone, and picked it up that his enemies were withstood. The fresh jawbone illustrates the importance of a "now" word from God; a "rhema word," as it were, that is fresh and vital and faith inspiring! With such a word, we can stand and fight for as long as necessary, until our enemies are piled up at our feet.

With the jawbone of a donkey, heaps upon heaps, with the jawbone of a donkey I have slain a thousand men!
Judges 15:16

Vigilant, Focused and Attentive

God's Word is settled forever in Heaven (Psalm 119:89), and when settled in our hearts, it will produce the faith and power to get results. We must be vigilant, however, as well as focused and attentive as we approach His Word. A superficial attitude, or an indifferent "take-it-or-leave-it" approach to the Word of God will prompt very little action from the Holy Spirit, or from the holy angels who stand ready to "hearken unto the voice of His Word" (Psalm 103:20).

Conversely, attitudes of reverence, humility and delight over the anointed Word, will garner tremendous results! Faith literally will explode in the hearts of those responding hungrily and appreciatively to the truth they hear or read, and this will prompt much activity in the spiritual realm. The common people, coming to Jesus "to *hear* and be healed of their diseases" (Luke 5:15; 6:17), never went away disappointed. As they heard Him speak, faith for the miraculous soared in their hearts, and God's power easily went into action. For these people, the combined action of the Holy Spirit and the mighty angels was vibrant and unabashed.

Watch Jesus to Know Father's Will

In an attempt to correct confusion concerning God's will, Jesus asked one of His disciples, "Have I been with you so long, and yet you have not known Me, Philip? *He who has seen Me has seen the Father*; so how can you say, 'Show us the Father?'" (John 14:9). Beloved, if we want to know God's will, as it relates to any number of concerns, we should watch the Scriptures closely to see what Jesus does. As "the express image of [God's] person," Jesus is literally the will of God in action! (See Hebrews 1:3.) That is why it is important for us to read and study the four gospels, indeed, the entire New Testament, for an accurate portrayal of God's heart for the sick and downtrodden. In it we see His will concerning many other situations as well.

Jesus sent the Holy Spirit to both unveil and empower the Word of God for us. If we will study it, and lean hard on the truth we find therein, the Holy Spirit will release great power as we pray and believe. But if we choose to remain ignorant, we will live in spiritual darkness and experience great lack. Therefore, it really comes down to this: How badly do we want to see God's hand impact the earth? And what price are we willing to pay to be vessels of this power? Like Job's friends, most people are satisfied in their ignorance. Most people are content to believe things that are inconsistent with God's Word. But you are different, friend! If you weren't, you would not have been drawn to this book. Something inside you desperately wants to know and experience the strong hand of the Lord in this hour. Something inside you wants to reject mediocrity when the electrifying power of the kingdom is within reach. Let us never settle for anything less than God's best! There is a higher level of life than what most Christians enjoy. There is a greater degree of power reserved for those who will embrace it.

Jesus' Significance

In the age we live in, the Father has given all things into the hand of His Son (John 3:35). Seated at the right hand of God, Jesus owns all authority in Heaven and on earth (Matthew 28:18), and will retain this authority until the last enemy—Death—is put completely under His feet (1 Corinthians 15:24-28).

Asaph saw this and prayed, "Let Your hand be upon the man of Your right hand, upon the son of man whom You made strong for Yourself" (Psalm 80:17). Jesus, the man of God's right hand, is indeed the strongest of all, upholding all things by the word of His power (Hebrews 1:3).

Of the Lord, Ethan rightly declared: "You have a mighty arm. Strong is your hand!" (Psalm 89:13). Like Job before him, he revered the One "in whose hand is the life of every living thing, and the breath of all mankind" (Job 12:10).

Being that agent by which He brings men out of bondage and death, the hand of the Lord is the manifesting power of the great King and Redeemer.

By strength of hand the Lord brought you out of this place.   Exodus 13:3

Any place or manner of bondage will yield its captives

if the hand of God is brought into action in a strong enough way. No sin, ignorance or sickness can stand up beneath the strong hand of the Lord when it manifests His glory.

> *And remember that ... the Lord your God brought you out ... by a mighty hand and by an outstretched arm.*
> Deuteronomy 5:15

When a person comes to God, Jesus alone has the ability to snatch him from the jaws of death and transport him into a glorious forever: "And I give them eternal life, and they shall never perish; neither shall anyone snatch them out of My hand" (John 10:28). Not only is His a saving hand, but it is also a *keeping* hand for the one who "stands by faith," and "holds fast to the word" of Christ's death, burial and resurrection (See Romans 11:20-22; 1 Corinthians 15:2-4.)

All hail the One who was, and is, and is to come! All hail the power of Jesus' name! Hats off to the strength of His awesome hand!

3
Extending the Kingdom

The early disciples understood the significance of God's hand for extending the kingdom. Early on they learned that unless God's hand came upon it, and provided the wind to fill its sails, the young ship of Zion would sit dead in the water. Lifting their voice to God with one accord, they cried: "Now, Lord...grant to your servants that with all boldness they may speak Your word, *by stretching out Your hand to heal,* and that signs and wonders may be done through the name of Your holy Servant Jesus" (Acts 4:24, 30). They requested boldness to preach the gospel despite persecution. They requested God to stretch forth His hand in signs, wonders and miracles, knowing that if He refused to release a miracle flow, they would fail in the task of world evangelism. What was the immediate outcome of this prayer for God's mighty hand? Acts 4:31 records, "The place where they were assembled together was shaken!" This indicates God's own "Amen!" to their request. And what was the long-term outcome? Acts 5:12 and 14 say, "And through the hands of the apostles many signs and wonders were done among the people...and believers were increasingly added to the Lord, multitudes of both men and women." What makes us think that we can get by on anything less than the strong hand of the Lord as we seek to gather the end time harvest?

He Used Their Hands

As the Lord stretched forth His hand to heal and add to the Church, He was pleased to use the hands of His apostles. But it wasn't long before the hands of other believers—ordinary but devoted believers—were also being used as instruments of His healing power. (See Acts 6:8; 8:5-7; 9:17.) In this way the early disciples truly co-labored with Christ, many times accomplishing impossible things. Each time one of them reached forth to bless or bring healing to someone in need, he understood his own hand to be an extension of the powerful hand of the One he represented, the One for whom he was an ambassador. Each time a believer reached forth to lay hands on a fevered brow or a leprous forehead, his hands became weapons through which the Spirit could release a powerful charge of resurrection power.

A Doctrine

The doctrine of the laying on of hands (Hebrews 6:3) was widely taught and practiced by the Church immediately following Jesus' ascension. Just prior to ascending into Heaven, Jesus commissioned His disciples with these words: "These signs will follow those who believe: In my name...*they will lay hands on the sick,* and they will recover" (Mark 16:17-18). This method of imparting God's healing power to sick bodies became a normal practice as the early Christians spread the gospel throughout the known world. For example, it is recorded that "God worked unusual miracles by the hands of Paul" as he established a thriving church in Ephesus (see Acts 19:11).

Besides being instruments through which the Lord can impart healing power and blessing, the hands can also be used to impart an anointing for special service in the kingdom. (See Acts 13:1-3.) Often, until sanctified hands are laid on someone who is called to special service, something will be lacking as they seek to carry out their responsibilities.

The laying on of hands also establishes a point of contact; it becomes a key juncture in time, at which God's minister *and* the one(s) prayed for release faith for what is needed. Impartation of divine graces occur through such physical contact *when* faith is present, hearts are right, and hindrances are absent.[1]

He Trains My Hands for War

He teaches my hands to make war, so that my arms can bend a bow of bronze.

Psalm 18:34

Blessed be my Rock, who trains my hands for war, and my fingers for battle.

Psalm 144:1

Before slinging the stone that felled the giant, David's fingers strummed the harp that "enthroned the Lord" (Psalm 22:3), and brought down the glory. Before raising the sword that slaughtered his enemies, he raised adoring hands in praise to his God. The former actions made possible the latter. Unfettered praise and worship always produces unfettered and skilled spiritual warriors.

Praise: An Act of War

Using our hands in praise to God is viewed as a spiritual act of aggression by Satan's kingdom. When God's high praises fill our mouths, and His two-edged sword fills our hands, spiritual forces are released that execute vengeance and punishment on our enemies, binding their nobles with chains and fetters of iron (see Psalm 149:6-9). Praise actually releases angels to do what we cannot! It has the ability to throw off the principalities and powers ranged against us. When the cymbals clash and the ram's horn blows, hell shudders. When the people shout and dance before the King, lifting up their best praises to the God of creation, the sound creates confusion in the enemy's ranks! We may not know all the mechanics of this spiritual law, but we know that our praise has far reaching consequences. That is why Satan resists it so vehemently.

My wife overheard a severely demonized man in a local market one day. He had never been inside our church, and yet was complaining bitterly to the lady behind the counter.

"They blow trumpets in that church," he growled, "and they yell, 'We triumph over you!' Oh, I hate that church!"

The trumpets about which the man spoke are shofars, or, ram's horns from Israel; and yes, we do sometimes shout, "We triumph over you!" It is funny that a man who had never darkened the door of our church knew what we did in our praise and worship services. People of praise and spiritual warfare develop a reputation with the demons of their region. I am sure the demonic gossip lines buzz every time some churches congregate to praise the Lord. May we all give the demons even more to gripe and complain about in coming days!

Strong Barriers

Two of the most formidable and unforgiving barriers for some Christians to break through, where praise is concerned, are the barriers of pride and fear. I have seen good men and women, who could be gallant warriors for God, stopped dead in their tracks at the base of these frowning obstacles. When pride and/or fear are strong, the captives appear to have an unseen spiritual substance gluing them to their seats, making it impossible to mount up in abandoned praise. Their feet seem locked in invisible cement, and their whole posture is rigid and confined. Such oppression often binds their arms to their sides, or crosses them over their chest, which is a posture of reticence. The oppression also covers their faces with darkness, sadness and gloom—and sometimes anger. Emotionless prisoners like these never know their potential as warriors until they break through these barriers and become worship warriors!

When Christians lift their hands in praise to God, clap them together in rhythm to a song, wave a banner, prophetically play an instrument, or use them in prophetic gesture, a certain dynamic is released! Our hands and fingers become primary tools of faith and expression, engaging the power of God and frustrating the purposes of Satan. Where David's hands were trained to handle the sling, the bow, or the sword, ours are trained to be lifted to God in praise, to bring healing to the sick, and to minister to the needs of those who need our help.

God's Hand Produces Fear

When the peoples of the earth learn that the hand of the Lord is relevant and mighty, they will learn to fear Him. Joshua, the great leader who took Israel into the Promised Land, made a powerful statement when the people passed through the Jordan River's parted waters.

Recalling an earlier deliverance from certain death through the waters of the Red Sea, Joshua cited an overall reason for such miracles: "That all the peoples of the earth may know *the hand of the Lord,* that it is mighty, that you may *fear* the Lord your God forever" (Joshua 4:24, author's emphasis).

From this we see that the hand of God produces three undeniable results: Firstly, it provides escape from certain destruction, as seen in Israel's deliverance from an enraged Egyptian Pharaoh. Secondly, it provides the means by which God's people are enabled to cross over into their inheritance. This was seen as the Israelites passed through the Jordan River and into the Promised Land. And thirdly, miracles become the means by which a great and widespread fear of the Lord is produced in the hearts of the people involved, as well as in the hearts of those who witness or hear of the miracles. This fear is always the result of the miraculous power of God.

When the hand of the Lord came on Ananias and Sapphira in judgment (Acts 5:1-11), "great fear came upon all the church and upon all who heard these things." And so we can see that when God's hand is witnessed in forms of

25

judgment or in showers of blessing, it will force men to face the reality of a God to whom all men are accountable.

In my novel, *Invisible Wilderness,* frontier revivalist, Andrew Woodlief, takes bold measures to arrest the attention of the careless and dull-hearted people of Welton, a village deep in the heart of the Appalachian Mountains. In order to do this, he locates the region's most impossible case, a young demon-possessed man who lives a mile or so south of town at the edge of the vast wilderness. With Holy Spirit boldness and power, and before several leading citizens of Welton, Andrew aggressively confronts and expels the demons tormenting the young man, and sets him gloriously free. This bold display of spiritual power does what it was designed to do: it gets the undivided attention of everybody in the vicinity. Awakening then breaks out, and hundreds of people are saved.

Beloved, a religion that talks of God's power, but never displays it, contradicts itself. Christianity should always display the miraculous, for as men and women see demonstrations of Holy Ghost power, they are more easily convinced that the word we preach is the genuine message given from God to man. (See 1 Corinthians 4:19-20.)

God's Hand Molds Us

Another work of God's hand is that of molding and shaping us into the Christians we need to be. Nevertheless, we each must yield to the pressure His hands apply. Peter exhorted us: "Therefore humble yourselves under the mighty hand of God, that He may exalt you in due time" (5:6). When the Master Potter puts force against parts of our lives, we must not rebel and question His wisdom and ability. Israel resisted the Lord's creative hand in this way, and it prolonged their time on the Potter's wheel. The prophet declared, "Woe to him who strives with his Maker! Shall the clay say to Him who forms it, 'What are you making?' Or shall your handiwork say, 'He has no hands?'" (Isaiah 45:9).

When we strive with our Maker, we are, in essence, saying, "What do You think You're doing with my life? I don't believe this is best for me. Your hand is not good, so take me off the wheel!"

But the relentless Potter continues doing what seems best to Him:

"O house of Israel, can I not do with you as this potter?" says the Lord.
"Look, as the clay is in the potter's hand, so are you in My hand, O house of Israel!"

Jeremiah 18:6

Professional potters have strong and gifted hands. So does our God. He throws each of us onto His wheel of development, sprinkles clean water on us, and begins applying a frightening amount of pressure to areas of our lives that need improvement. He is determined to shape us into vessels that can hold water and glorify His name. We do not choose what part of us He is to work on at any given moment, that's His decision. "Here, Lord," we may pray, "work on improving my financial situation." But God says, "No, I'm going to work on another part for awhile! I am going to work on your character!" The Lord is always more concerned with our character than He is with our comfort.

Allow me to construct a brief allegory for you to illustrate my point: A Christian building contractor finds himself on the Potter's wheel. As you will see, no one ever ends up on the wheel when he thinks he is ready for it; it always happens when God decides.

On Monday the contractor learns that a client who owes him ten thousand dollars will be unable to pay him for at least two more weeks. This unwanted information creates tension for the contractor, because he himself has creditors who are demanding payment for what he owes them, and he has employees who need to be paid. The pressure begins to mount. Throughout the night, the fretful contractor tosses and turns on his bed, unable to get a wink of sleep.

Early on Tuesday morning, as the sleep-deprived man wanders into the laundry room to find a clean pair of kakis, he discovers that his daughter's new puppy has pulled clothes from the hamper and chewed-up two pairs of new socks. Immediately he must overcome the urge to drop kick the pup into the next county. His Christlike nature is sorely challenged.

Once on the job that morning, he learns that one of his best carpenters has decided to work for another builder. "He's gonna pay me more per hour," the turncoat boasts, "and there are better benefits." Emotional pressure intensifies.

The next couple of days level out somewhat, and in spite of the fact that the client hasn't paid him his ten grand yet, he starts feeling a bit better. But then it happens! The motor in his backhoe blows up…and so does he! After ranting and raving for several minutes, he jumps in his truck and heads for home, embarrassed that he had a temper tantrum in front of his crew, all men he's been trying to win to the Lord. While driving down the highway, shame blushing his face, he remembers how a month ago the thought came to him, again and again, "I need to have my mechanic see about that strange pinging in the motor of my backhoe." He realizes the Lord had been trying to head off this disaster, but he hadn't responded correctly. It is his fault and no one else's.

That night, the beleaguered contractor tosses and turns fitfully, unable to put his troubles from his mind. Finally, at three o'clock in the morning, he drags himself from his warm bed and forces himself downstairs to the den.

"Oh, God!" he sobs, as he stretches out on the floor, his face in his hands. "I feel like such a jerk! Such a failure! Such a loser! Help me, please! I can't take much more of this! I ought to just sell out and get a job down at the factory!"

As the hour passes, God begins speaking to His man about forgiveness, the need to forgive his creditors, the need to forgive people when they let him down. He needs to forgive the carpenter who went to work for another builder, and he even needs to forgive his own daughter for bringing that darned puppy home.

The Lord also talks to him about trust. "How will I be able to bless you later if you won't trust Me now?" the Lord asks.

After communing with God for an hour or more, the man returns to his bed unburdened and refreshed. Although he only gets a couple hours of sleep before he has to get up, he finds that God has prepared him for the new day with a new and better attitude. Moments before leaving the house, the phone rings, and it is the man who owes him ten thousand dollars. "I'll come by your house tonight with check in hand," the caller promises, "and I have a list of some other projects I want you to do for me. Thank you for your patience."

"Patience!" the contractor chuckles to himself. "If you only knew."

For several days the Potter's hand had applied pressure to the man's life in order to mold into him essential, godly qualities that would make him more like Christ. It wasn't comfortable, and it wasn't fun. And it certainly wasn't what he would have chosen to go through at the time. But in the end, God accomplished what He wanted to accomplish. Such pressure is often necessary if one ever hopes to become an earthen vessel that can carry God's glory to the people around him.

Prepared Beforehand

For we are His workmanship, created in Christ Jesus for good works, which God prepared beforehand that we should walk in them.   Ephesians 2:10

As Christians, we are not the ones to choose what *we* want to be and do in life. We must allow God to make those choices for us. Because He knows what is best for us, we show wisdom when we seek His direction. As we walk with Him, His desires become our own, and He works within our hearts both to will and to do His good pleasure (Philippians 2:13).

One man may want to be a pastor, but God wants him to be a schoolteacher instead. Another man may want to be a schoolteacher, but God wants him to be a pastor. As a pastor, the one called to be a schoolteacher would fall short; and as a schoolteacher, the one called and gifted to be a pastor would fall short. Each may be able to function at a certain level of success as he stubbornly attempts to do what he is not called to do, but God's best purposes for his life will never be realized. He will discover that he comes up short in one or more key areas of his own chosen occupation. However, if God has called him to a certain occupation, He will equip him with everything he needs to succeed wonderfully in that calling. Without the call of God to a particular profession, we discover an undying frustration as we struggle to accomplish things in our own power and wisdom! Concerning certain ministers of his day, Jeremiah wrote, "I have not sent these prophets, *yet* they ran" (23:21). And what was the outcome? These self-sent prophets missed God's mark for the people, and true revival never happened (v. 22).

The validity of a prophet's ministry is not based merely on what he says to the people, but rather, it is based on God's call on his life. If God has not called him, then he comes under false pretenses. If the Lord has not commissioned him, he comes without Heaven's authorization. And if he comes without Heaven's authorization, there will be no genuine power. How can a man know the difference? I believe he must first "make his calling sure," or be sure of his calling. (See 2 Peter 1:10.) If he is truly called, there will be an accompanying authority, and with it, an anointing to make him successful. People will respond to his ministry. Not all responses will be good, but there will be a positive response by those who have an ear to hear what the Spirit is saying through the man.

I believe that unless God clearly shows him otherwise, each man should only enter realms where his calling leads him. A man's calling and its attending talents will make room for him, and bring him before the right people at the right times. (See Proverbs 18:16.) As a rule, every believer should get in touch with what stirs his heart, makes him tick, and with what comes naturally to him. He should be comfortable in his own skin. He should ask himself and those closest to him, "Do other people recognize my calling for life and ministry, or am I stubbornly trying to see what isn't there? Do others receive easily from me, or am I trying to force myself on them?" Honest friends and leaders can help us here. If we don't have some measure of gifting for what we are trying to do, then it will become obvious and odious to everybody upon whom we try to force it. If no one is receiving from us, beloved, it is probably because we are neither called nor equipped by God to do what we are trying to do. Since God qualifies the called, we should humble ourselves under His hand, accept our calling, and flow in the gifts He gives in concert with His call.

Smith Wigglesworth was asked to chair a missions conference during his later years. At one of the meetings, a missionary who was not anointed to address large crowds attempted to take more time than what he was gifted for. After droning on for several miserable minutes, Wigglesworth, known for his candor, stood to his feet and bawled, "My God, man, sit down, you're killing us!"

Suppose someone said something like that every time you forced yourself into a position where you don't belong. How would you handle it? It may hurt your feelings for a while, but it would keep you out of areas where your calling hasn't led you. When we attempt to step into ministries where our calling has not carried us, we actually bring a measure of death to a work rather than an abundant supply of life. We need to know and accept that!

There are times when overseeing a local church is an unpleasant responsibility. At such times I think I would rather go on the road and do concerts like Phil Keaggy. But God has neither called nor gifted me with the talent to do that. If I were to try to do it anyway, people would not be blessed and neither would I. You see, regardless of how much I wish I could play the guitar and travel like Phil Keaggy, I am still called to be a local pastor, and not a concert guitarist! I accept the fact that my full potential as a guitarist will only be realized in eternity and not in this life. Therefore, I am content to live with who and what I really am. For now I am a pastor, and I embrace that calling with gratitude.

A Genuine Calling Produces a Genuine Stirring

Exodus 35:26 says, "And all the women *whose hearts stirred with a skill* spun yarn of goats' hair." True God-given skills (not just desires) should stir our hearts to legitimate calling and action. Our God-given skills, not self-serving desires, are what make room for us in life. Our self-serving desires often are born out of dissatisfaction with who we are, or what we are called to do. But it is our skills that tell us who we really are.

Exodus 36:1 says, "So Bezalel, Aholiab, and every *skilled* person to whom *the Lord has given skill* and ability to *know how* to carry out all the work of constructing the sanctuary, shall do according to all that the Lord has commanded" (NIV). God-given skills and aptitudes are essential for the productive building of individual lives, businesses, and the Church.

While building the wilderness tabernacle, artisans called and gifted by God were given specific tasks based on

32

their God-given talents. I believe this is the basic principle by which the Lord calls and anoints men and women today. Miserable indeed is one who tries to make God bless what he is neither gifted nor anointed to do. When the hand tries to be a foot, everything is thrown off balance. When the eye tries to ingest food like a mouth, vision is impaired. If a man stops up his nose and tries to breathe through his ears, death will occur in a short period of time. Remember, Paul wrote, "For we are *His* workmanship, created in Christ Jesus for good works, which God prepared beforehand that we should walk in them" (Ephesians 2:10). Our goal is to discover what God has prepared for our lives, and then yield to His creative hand as He enables us to walk in our pre-ordained destinies. Even in suffering and hardship God is able to work in us a far more exceeding and eternal weight of glory if we will trust Him and not complain.

4
His Good Hand On Zerubbabel

If there was ever a time when the Jewish nation needed the strong hand of God's favor, it was while languishing in the land of Babylon for seventy years.

By the rivers of Babylon, there we sat down, yea, we wept when we remembered Zion. We hung our harps upon the willows in the midst of it. For there those who carried us away captive asked of us a song, and those who plundered us requested mirth, saying, "Sing us one of the songs of Zion!" How shall we sing the Lord's song in a foreign land?
Psalm 137:1-4

For decades the prophets had warned Israel and Judah to return to the Lord. But the people would not heed the warnings! And so, just as God had said, they were carried away into Babylonian captivity.

A Remnant

Even amidst the sorrow of Babylonian, and later, Persian domination, there was a remnant of prayer warriors who faithfully sought the God of Heaven for a restoration of all that had been stolen. The pure devotion of men like Daniel and his friends; the courage of Mordecai and Esther; and the passionate vision of Ezra and Nehemiah, did not go unnoticed by God. At the close of seventy years of captivity, the Lord began moving the hearts of Persian kings to allow a remnant of Jews to return to the land of their fathers. This "returning" was carried out in two main stages over the course of about six decades, and is termed "the second exodus" by many scholars. Although this return from captivity was not as impressive as when the whole nation of Israel was delivered from Egypt by a display of God's power, it was still as important to the plan of God. And where the strong, furious hand of God moved against Egypt to persuade Pharaoh to let the people go, the gentle hand of the Lord came upon Persian kings Cyrus, Darius, and Artaxerxes (Ezra 1:1-4; 4:24; 7:1, 13), persuading them to send the Jews back to Jerusalem to do all that was on their hearts.

Restoration Men

The little books of Ezra and Nehemiah tell of three devoted Jews—Zerubbabel, Ezra and Nehemiah—who each led a contingent of their countrymen from Babylon (then under Persian control) to Jerusalem to rebuild something for God. Not one of them was sent to create something that had never before existed, but to rebuild, recover and restore something precious that had been destroyed, stolen or lost. Zerubbabel was to re-lay the foundation of Solomon's temple, and erect a house where the Lord's people could again sacrifice to and worship the living God. Ezra arrived almost six decades later to restore proper forms of worship to Israel according to the patterns set down in the Law of Moses.[2] Eleven years into Ezra's ministry in Jerusalem, Nehemiah appeared. With the blessing of Persia's king, his task was to rebuild the crumbling walls around the Holy City (which he did in just fifty-two days), and support Ezra in the task of reviving and reforming the people of God within the city.

Before examining the verses that speak of the hand of the Lord on Ezra and Nehemiah, let us consider that the hand of the Lord was first on Zerubbabel, the man who led the original group back to Jerusalem.

God's Hand on Zerubbabel

With the blessing of Cyrus, first king of Persia, Zerubbabel led the initial contingent of workers to Jerusalem, a body of 42,360 Jews upon "whose spirits God had moved"

(Ezra 1:5). They came to resettle the cities of Israel, and to rebuild the temple Nebuchadnezzar's armies had destroyed in Jerusalem (2:64, 70). Each man's vision dovetailed into that which God had given Zerubbabel, and they were eager to follow his lead toward the fulfillment of a corporate dream. A lesson for today's leaders is found in this, and that is this: never attempt to build closely with people who have not experienced a stirring in their hearts for the vision God has given you! If their hearts have not been moved upon by the Holy Spirit, they may become your greatest detractors somewhere down the line, and you will rue the day that you included them in what God asked you to do. A wise leader, however, will look for the men and women God is sending him, and look for ways to use their unique gifts and talents. He will also appreciate the unique visions God has placed in the hearts of those called to serve with him, and if he can blend their visions with his own, he will seek to do so. A leader who only seeks to impose his own vision on the people is a fool with tunnel vision. He should be recognizing, assisting and releasing the visionaries around him who carry their own special heartbeat for ministry. There are powerful deliverance ministers sitting quietly in the pews of many churches whose gifts are never recognized and encouraged by their pastors. Likewise, there are prophets and evangelists who never receive the encouragement they need to step out and impact nations. But here is a warning: While the many different callings, and the wide assortment of spiritual and motivational gifts found in the body of Christ should be encouraged and used to advance the kingdom, personal vision and ambition that works crosswise to, or out-of-step with a ministry's overall vision, should be avoided. God gives His leaders the prerogative to decide who, when, where and how to blend the various visions in his church or ministry into one unified force that will impact the nations.

Zerubbabel knew to include the right people in his

mission; he only wanted those whom God was calling. While he did not personally handpick over 42,000 teammates, he did choose faithful men who were able to assist him in this process. It is obvious that Zerubbabel was highly administrative, and could superintend a massive undertaking that involved huge numbers of people.

Although no particular verse states that God's hand was on Zerubbabel for rebuilding the temple at Jerusalem, it is obvious that God's good hand was present or he would not have been able to accomplish all he did. The Scripture does say that "the eye of their God" was on the elders of the Jews (those who supported Zerubbabel), so that, once in Jerusalem, the corrupt city officials could not make them turn from their mission (Ezra 5:5). Civil detractors failed in their resistance to the rebuilding of the temple because God's gracious eye was indeed on the elders, and His hand was on the righteous builders. In the days facing the Church, let us pray that the "eye of our God" will be on us as we build together. Let us pray that the enemy's plans to discourage and defeat us will fail, and that God's plans to prosper us will succeed.

Shadow of the Apostolic

Zerubbabel's party of workers was an Old Testament "type" or "shadow" of New Testament apostolic ministry. This special builder did not function on his own, but employed, as we have seen, a team of anointed co-laborers who accompanied him to Jerusalem. Standing at his side, much as Silas and Timothy stood at the side of the apostle Paul, were several men of significant gifting. (See Ezra 2:2; 3:9.) A brief study of each of their names suggests the strengths they might have added to the group. I am sure there were many times when Zerubbabel felt like quitting, but these men stood firm with the support he needed to keep pressing ahead. People like this mean as much to an apostle as a master sergeant does to a commander on the battlefield. They are indispensable heroes - unsung but priceless workhorses in the kingdom of God.

Jeshua was the man who seems to have been closest to Zerubbabel. His name appears often in Ezra, and means, "Yahweh is salvation." It is very likely that God used Jeshua to provide important insight and encouragement at times when it seemed like everything they were doing was failing. Certainly, at times, he was a manifestation of God's saving, redeeming power to Zerubbabel.

Nehemiah was another faithful member of the team. This was not the man whose book follows Ezra's, but was a man who was part of Zerubbabel's lineup of exiles returning to Jerusalem. His name means "comforted by Jehovah." It is not hard to guess what his motivational gift was, and how he benefited everyone when they needed consolation and encouragement, much as Barnabas, whose name means "son of consolation," brought comfort to those with whom he ministered during the days of the early Church. (See Acts 4:36-37; 9:26-28; 2 Corinthians 8:18-19.)

Seraiah was the third man listed as one of Zerubbabel's co-workers. His name means "soldier of Jehovah." There is no doubt about this man's interests. There has to be at least one spiritual warfare enthusiast on every apostolic team, and I feel sure that Seraiah was the man. Although *spiritual* warfare was not something Old Testament saints knew much about, the heartbeat of many Jews was spiritually militant. Elisha knew of angelic ministry (2 Kings 6:15-17), so it is likely he knew the nature of demonic work as well. If anyone on Zerubbabel's team entered into prayer warfare against demonic resistance to the rebuilding of the temple, it was probably Seriah, soldier of Jehovah.

A fellow by the name of Reelaiah was also included in Zerubbabel's lineup of workers, and his name means "Jehovah has caused to tremble." The reverence for God and His Law possessed by this man was probably second to none.

A person like Reelaiah has the uncanny ability to draw everyone around him back to the written Word when he sees them beginning to drift. I would guess that whenever the Law of God was read to the people, Reelaiah would tremble with respect and awe.

A builder named Bilshan was also on the team, and he had a very interesting meaning attached to his name. His name meant "son of the tongue." Obviously this man was a gifted orator, eloquent and very persuasive in speech. I feel sure his anointed support and faith-inspiring fusillades strengthened his fellow-workers when they were in need of encouragement. There are men and women among us today whose very presence and personality lifts us whenever we are with them.

Bigvai was there as well. His name means "happy or fortunate." The name comes from *baga,* meaning, "good luck." Some people seem to have charmed lives, although it has nothing to do with charm or good luck. God is the one who bestows His favor on his children. They seem to have "the Midas touch." Everything they touch seems to turn to gold.

Rehum, whose name means "merciful," was also with Zerubbabel. When facing men of questionable character, this man probably erred on the side of mercy if he erred at all. His merciful nature probably prevented the black and white "prophet-types" from bringing judgment down on the heads of those who irritated them.

Baanah, whose name means "son of affliction," also graced this special lineup of builders. When people band together to do something for the Lord, waves of persecution and affliction will beat against them. At such times, it is good to have experienced men and women around who know how to navigate the turbulent waters. Baanah's name represents the kind of leadership that knows how to plow through tribulation's rough seas. It stays calm when the tendency is to panic, because it has been through it before, and knows God to be faithful. "Many are the afflictions of the righteous, but the Lord delivers him out of them all" (Psalm 34:19). Baanah was confident of this fact.

Kadmiel was another member of Zerubbabel's team, and his name means, "El is first," or, "God is in the front." This name paints quite a picture! When Kadmiel was assured in his own heart that the Lord was out in front leading, he was bold to follow. We should all be this way. If we are not convinced that the Lord is leading the way into a significant undertaking, we should step back and wait for inward confirmation, no matter how much outward pressure we feel to proceed. Too often in the past I have moved into something based on the strong reasoning of men, and not on the word of the Lord, and it has cost me dearly. Kadmiel was also a man others would see out in front, blazing new trails for God and restoring paths to dwell in. His character likely mirrored the courage of the Lord to make up the vanguard of all He was doing in Jerusalem.

Another valuable asset to Zerubbabel's team was Judah, whose name means, "praise." Knowing that God is "enthroned in the praises of Israel" (Psalm 22:3), Judah dreamed of making the temple a place where Yahweh could take His rightful place. The spirit of Judah is among God's builders today, "silencing the voice of the enemy and avenger" (see Psalm 8:2). Anointed praise has proven to be a most valuable part in restoring New Testament Christianity to the world today.

Henadad was another valuable man connected to Zerubbabel's team. His name means, "a deity is gracious," or "favor of Hadad." This man probably lived and breathed a grace that refreshed all who worked near him. It is joy to work beside a person who is full of mercy and grace, and who always looks for the best in you.

The Prophetic Connection

Not only did Zerubbabel have the support of these faithful and talented temple builders, but the anointed vocal ministries of two powerful prophets also encouraged him: Haggai and Zechariah. The name Haggai means "festive," and Zechariah means "Yahweh has remembered." As Zerubbabel and his team labored on the foundation, these two men prophesied to the Jews in Judah and Jerusalem, giving the encouragement needed to persevere in spite of adversaries who opposed the rebuilding process. Ezra 5:2 says, "the prophets of God were with them, *helping them.*" Genuine prophets, when connected to apostles, should benefit and not diminish the important work being done. I appreciate the comment in Ezra 6:14 concerning their activity: "So the elders of the Jews *built,* and *they prospered* through the prophesying of Haggai the prophet and Zechariah the son of Iddo." Hallelujah!

Zechariah's father, Iddo, whose name means "timely," represents the faithfulness of God to produce a prophet for a crucial time of rebuilding. I shudder to think of the outcome had Haggai and Zechariah not been received by the team. The supportive role prophets are to play in apostolic work must never be downplayed or ignored. Oh, that the true prophets of God would come forth in this hour to encourage those who build the Church in hostile environments!

By the mighty hand of the Lord, Zerubbabel was at last able to complete and dedicate the temple in Jerusalem. Indeed, "the righteous and the wise *and* their works are in the hand of God" (Ecclesiastes 9:1). When God's builders are persistent and remain committed to the work of restoration, the time comes when all things are completed and the Lord releases a joy among the faithful that is beyond comprehension.

A Summary of Chapter Four

As we close this chapter, let us review the key points that show how the hand of the Lord was on Zerubbabel, and how we too can experience this blessing.

1. When the hand of the Lord is on a visionary leader, God will quicken the spirit of those in positions of power (secular or religious), prompting them to favor and support him. King Cyrus of Persia favored Zerubbabel and eagerly sent him to rebuild the temple in Jerusalem. (See Ezra 1:1-5.) If you are a Christian with vision, allow time for the Lord to sanction it with the favor of those with proper authority. Step out and push an agenda without their "amen" (if the Lord tells you to wait for it), and you will fall on your face and suffer without their help.

2. When the hand of the Lord is on a visionary leader, there will be other people to encourage him "with articles of silver and gold…and with precious things" (Ezra 1:6). A project instituted by God will not lack the resources necessary to complete the job.

3. When the hand of the Lord is on a visionary leader, God will cause anointed and gifted people to rally around him and assist in the work being done (1:5; 2:2). If God does not move on someone's spirit to rise up and help, we shouldn't want them. Such a person might become a detractor.

4. When the foundation of the temple was completed, there was cause for great rejoicing among the Jews (3:10-13). Foundations are very important to the purposes of God and should cause us to rejoice when they are completed.

5. Zerubbabel and his builders were only sanctioned to rebuild the house of the Lord, and that is all they were trying to do.

However, their adversaries, upon seeing the foundation of the temple completed, accused the Jews of trying to rebuild the entire city as a Jewish stronghold. As a result of this, the new Persian king, Artaxerxes Smerdis, stopped the Jews dead in their tracks, and halted even the rebuilding of the temple, which had been sanctioned by his predecessor, Cyrus. (See 4:11-24.) In time, however, Artaxerxes Smerdis passed from the scene (God removed him), and Darius replaced him. With the blessing of this new king, Zerubbabel was released to resume rebuilding the temple. What does this teach us? If we are patient, and commit our work to the Lord, He will remove the wicked who resist our work, and replace them with men and women of a more amiable nature.

6. A visionary leader with God's hand upon him should value the encouragement that comes through prophetic ministries. Zerubbabel and the elders of the Jews who built, "prospered through the prophesying of Haggai and Zechariah" (6:14). It seems the prophets were nowhere around when the foundation was being laid during the initial burst of building. But once Darius came to power and released the Jews to resume construction on the temple, the prophets Haggai and Zechariah were in place, energizing and encouraging the great work being done (5:1).

7. Prophetic ministry that genuinely helps apostolic builders will be "with them" in the building process (Ezra 5:2). They will be with them in heart, vision, purpose and commitment, and not abandon them when things get tough. Fly-by-night prophets, whose hearts are neither with the builders nor committed to the work being done, are a scourge to true kingdom builders. Who needs them? Who wants them?

8. When a genuine God-ordained work is being done, "the eye of the Lord" will be on the builders, safeguarding their

work, and seeing it through to completion (5:5).

9. When the temple was completed, the people who had "separated themselves from the filth of the nations" in order to seek the Lord (6:21-22), kept the Feast of Unleavened Bread for seven days with joy. Joy should be an earmark of restoration! As a result of this, the Lord changed the heart of an old enemy, the king of Assyria, and turned it toward the Jews. This king began to strengthen their hand, helping them to complete the temple. Indeed, when a man's ways please the Lord, He makes even his enemies to be at peace with him. What does this tell you and me? Just simply stay the course, and keep doing what you know God has called you to do. Leave to God all the petty arguments raised by the adversaries, and He will either change them or remove them.

5
Essential Foundations Restored Today

When Zerubbabel's work of laying the foundation was completed, it gave cause for great rejoicing among the Jews in Israel, in fact, when the builders were finished, all the people took part in a praise and worship service that would have impressed Paul Wilber. (See Ezra 3:10-13.) Such a reaction to the laying of the temple's foundation reveals the importance of proper foundations to the heart of God. Without them, everything we build is in eminent danger of collapse. This is true of individual lives, families, churches, communities and nations.

Two essential foundations needing restoration today are anointed discipleship and apostolic authority. Whenever these two foundation stones are missing, a brand of Christianity results that is both flawed and powerless. Take discipleship for instance. When a person is born again, he must quickly be established on the proper spiritual foundations or he will languish. Essential foundation stones are the Word of God, a life of prayer, and fellowship with believers of like precious faith. In the Word, one learns the classical Christian doctrines so necessary for a well-rounded understanding of God. In prayer, he maintains vital, fresh contact with the Father, and receives infusions of strength so he can stand in tribulation and not lose heart. In fellowship he gets the warm-blooded, face-to-face contact with God through His body that is so essential for growth. If he is not placed on these foundations he will not grow and develop properly.

Practical Discipleship

When carried out properly, discipleship requires a whole lot of time and a deep level of commitment. Both he who is mentored and the one doing the mentoring *must* be committed to the time, money and energy involved in doing a thorough job. My home is a Grand Central for many of the believers in our fellowship—particularly the younger ones who are still getting established in the faith. These young ones pretty much come and go as they please. We feed them, counsel them, teach them the Word, and give them refuge in our home. Whether they are receiving counsel and ministry or are simply lounging around fellowshipping with other believers, we want them to feel welcomed and a big part of who we are and what we're doing. God truly "sets the solitary in families." We want those allotted to our care and tutelage to feel important and safe, and so we open our home and share with them our lives. If you truly want to disciple others you must make room in your life, and even become addicted to hospitality. When Darlene and I are not entertaining and caring for the babes among us, we feel out-of-sorts with our calling. When they are around us, things naturally "click" in the spirit. Near us, they pick up our anointing through association, as well as through direct instruction. If we are ministering to someone in need, we get our young disciples to join us. By doing this they receive the hands on training essential for becoming able ministers of God's power. In more formal settings, such as in church services where we are ministering to the needy, we include our most faithful disciples. We enjoy turning them loose to minister in our prayer lines, and listen with satisfaction as they lay hands on the sick, cast out demons, or speak God-given words of knowledge to the ones standing before them. We have seen miracles occur as their young faith goes to work against the difficult situations some of those people bring to the prayer lines.

The school of the prophets conducted by prophets Elijah and Elisha, was more than a rigid classroom setting. It involved many field trips, included hands-on training, and it required that the disciples have a fairly close relationship with their mentors. This was also how it was with Jesus and His disciples. Discipleship should be no less today!

No Excuses

Jesus commissioned the Church to "make disciples of all nations" (Matthew 28:19), not simply lead people to Christ. Far too many decisions for Christ fail to flourish as true conversions simply because no one takes discipleship seriously.

When one has truly received Jesus as his Lord and Savior, he should immediately place himself under God's Word, submitting his spiritual development to the oversight of mature men and women who can establish him in truth, guard him from error, and secure him in Christ's fold. Although churches should provide different levels and modes of discipleship, new converts are responsible to take advantage of what is offered. When a new believer backslides for lack of nourishment and care, we should not be so quick to blame the church, unless of course, the church has offered nothing to help him grow in his faith. Each new believer has the personal responsibility to join the family of God at the corporate dinner table, and not isolate himself in the bedroom of self-centeredness like an ill-tempered teenaged boy or girl who rejects the family. I am tired of seeing the Church take the rap for a convert's failure to grow in God—particularly in America. No nation on earth offers so much to young Christians. Dynamic teaching is available at the click of a button. Some of the best foundational material available is sold in Christian bookstores across the nation. Churches exist in almost every neighborhood of every city. Pastors, elders, and mature saints are eager to help the spiritual babes grow. If they truly want to grow and prosper in their faith, everything they need is available if they will only look around a bit, and take advantage of what is offered.

When I was saved I didn't need anybody to beg me to come to fellowship. Instead, I sought it out. Because I was hungry to learn more about the wonderful Savior I had just received, I thought nothing of taking the time or spending the money to get closer to Him. I well remember calling a local Methodist pastor and asking him if there was a Bible study I could attend. Within weeks I was in regular attendance at a simple, straightforward Bible study that helped me take those early first steps toward an overcoming Christian life. Before long, the cash I spent on pornography and cartons of beer began to be spent on teaching tapes, books, and Christian music albums. I couldn't get enough of the Word. The Bible exhorts us to "buy the truth, and do not sell it, also wisdom and instruction and understanding" (Proverbs 23:23). One year I was blowing hard earned dollars on rock concerts and the next year I was spending hard-earned dollars on believers' conventions! A radical and undeniable transformation was underway and everybody could see it. The hunger that gnawed at my heart, as well as an ever-increasing, insatiable spiritual thirst, demanded that I feed and quench them with the marvelous things of God! Such spiritual cravings are placed in our hearts when we are born again so that we will turn our energies toward the Lord and begin to grow.

When natural babies are born in hospital delivery rooms, they soon begin to cry for their mothers' life-giving milk. They may not be able to understand this craving, but an instinctive hunger demands to be fed! If a newborn never shows a desire for momma's milk, it is probably sick, dying or dead. Many who make a hasty decision for Christ are like that. If they are only moved emotionally to voice the sinner's prayer, but don't consider the cost of commitment, they will probably experience a false start. However, if there is a genuine spiritual change in a person's heart when they pray for salvation, a gnawing spiritual hunger for the things of God will result, and they will grow before our very eyes.

True Conversions
Too often in Christianity we rush potential converts through to hasty decisions, not allowing the Word we preach the time to gestate fully. Thomas Boston, a sixteenth century English reformer, aptly described this problem in his book, *The Art of Man-Fishing*:

Wherefore, O my soul, if ever thou be taken up with an exercised conscience [someone you are trying to win to Christ], have a care that thou do not apply the cure before the wound be deep enough. Take all means to understand whether the soul be content to take Christ on His own terms or not. Alas! Many this way, by having the wound scurfed over, are rather killed than cured.[3]

Boston said, "Take all means to understand whether the soul be content to take Christ on His own terms or not." To take the Lord on His terms demands that the prospective convert grasp at least some understanding of what Christ demands in return for the gift of salvation. Jesus gave His life, that we might, in return, give Him our lives. "Repent," He said, "and believe the gospel!" (Mark 1:15). I need not expound on the word *repent,* but suffice it to say that simply believing in the Lord is not enough. One must turn from his wicked way and embark on a brand new journey with Christ at the head of his life. Some profound changes should be evident when one has truly been born again. The reality of the New Creation should take effect. True repentance is transforming power.

When William Carvosso ministered throughout England in the early 1800s, his practice was to wound people with the Law, and then heal them with grace. Before someone could genuinely repent and be saved, he reasoned, they would first need to grasp the fact that they were worthy of nothing but the wrath of a just and holy God. They needed to see that it was their sin, just as much as the next man's sin, that put Jesus on that cross. Cut to the heart and sobered by a stark realization of their own sinfulness, people would then be ready to do whatever was necessary to receive salvation and have their lives changed. Carvosso's personal memoirs reveal many instances where he ministered a heart-arresting word to people in their homes or businesses, only to leave them burdened beneath the Holy Spirit's convicting power.

A day or two later, he would return to examine their state of mind, and often find them in the throes of an unsettling conviction, literally weighed down with the enormity of their sinfulness before God. He would also find them desperate to gain the mercy and forgiveness Jesus Christ offers to all repentant souls. When these people prayed for salvation, they found it with great joy and appreciation, and remained true to their commitment for the rest of their mortal lives. We cannot say that about many people who pray to receive Christ today. I think we've made it a little too easy for them to become Christians. By not faithfully presenting the *demands* along with the promises of the gospel, too many stillborn babies are coming forth. Maybe we're pushing too hard. Maybe we're too busy totaling our numbers. Maybe we are too busy comparing ourselves to other Christian churches with their bloated membership rolls.

Beloved, your only responsibility to some people is to sow the seeds that will grow toward a harvest. Jesus said, "First the blade, then the ear, then the full corn in the ear—then the harvest!" (see Mark 4:28). Weeks, months and years can sometimes pass between the planting of a seed and the time of harvest. Therefore, let each of us realize that we are not called to win everyone the first time we speak with them. Maybe our only responsibility is to sow a seed, or perhaps water one already sown by another. If we can see ourselves as part of a chain of encounters people may need to experience before they can be harvested, it will help us not be discouraged when they seem uninterested, and it will also keep us from being too pushy. Maybe some folks need time to reflect and wrestle with God a little while as they come to grips with their own desperate need.

I led a woman to Christ the other day who wept her way into the kingdom. She was a desperate soul, haunted by the guilt of her own sinful condition and the mess she had made of her life. As I prayed with her, God made me aware that, while I was honored to lead her through the sinner's prayer, someone else had started the miracle by faithfully sowing the seeds of the gospel in her heart. I was simply stepping into an unfolding drama that had begun perhaps many years earlier. By the time God placed me before the woman, the seed had matured past the blade stage, past the ear stage, and had reached the full grain in the ear stage. That lady was ready to be harvested!

As we discussed the matters of Heaven and Hell, hers was not a flippant, take-Him-or-leave-Him response. She was not half-hearted or vacillating like so many others who are rushed through to hasty decisions. This woman knew that Jesus was her only hope for a blessed life here and eternal life in the hereafter. I would rather pray with one person like this than a thousand who have little awareness of their great need. Such a person can be brought successfully into the family of God and nurtured along to maturity.

The Apostolic Foundation

Not only is discipleship important to the ongoing development of an individual believer, but apostolic discipleship and oversight is also important to the ongoing growth and success of a young church or ministry. When a new work is being established, it is best that those with apostolic and prophetic authority oversee it. This doesn't mean that the visionary who began the work should abdicate his responsibilities, and hand everything over to an apostle, but it does mean he should safeguard the work by seeking proper oversight and counsel. Such authority helps to keep the work on track, insuring that the wrong elements (people, doctrines or activities) do not infiltrate to discourage the vision and derail the plan of God. Let us look at an example of what I mean.

When the people of Samaria received the Lord under the preaching of Philip (Acts 8), a dangerous sorcerer named Simon threatened to undermine all that had been accomplished in the fresh, new awakening. Philip may have been a powerful evangelist, but his spiritual credentials lacked the gifting needed to shield and establish the new work on all the proper foundations. A deceiver like Simon would find easy pickings if not stopped in his tracks. That is where the apostles came in. The Word says, "when the apostles who were at Jerusalem heard that Samaria had received the word of God, they sent Peter and John to them" (Acts 8:14). With apostolic anointing and piercing spiritual insight, these two men were able to carry the work at Samaria to the next level, which was witnessed as they baptized the new converts in the Holy Spirit, thereby releasing each one's potential for effective ministry. The apostles' special anointing was also evidenced as they exposed and confronted the deceptive motives of Simon. Who knows what might have happened had this evil man worked his way into leadership in the fledgling church? Who knows what crazy doctrines he would have come up with to pollute the pure current of God in that region? From the day the apostles Peter and John arrived in Samaria, the work at Samaria began to be placed on the proper foundations.

A Caution

Concerning apostolic and prophetic oversight for young or struggling churches or ministries, a caution is due. There are a number of people floating across the spiritual landscape, claiming to be apostles and prophets, but who have no solid proof to back their claims. In fact, if they have to tell you they are an apostle or a prophet, they probably are not!

A few years ago a man and his wife attended one of our Sunday morning meetings. Midway through the praise service he stood up and began to prophesy. What he said wasn't all that bad, but it lacked the touch of divine unction. My spiritual antenna went up, and I was prepared to stop him if he did it again.

After the morning's meeting, I greeted him out of courtesy.

"What's your name, brother?" I politely asked.

His reply was a dead give-away. "My name is brother D. I'm an apostle."

I didn't ask him *what* he was; I asked him *who* he was.

"What church do you belong to?" I prodded.

"Oh, I don't belong to any particular church. I'm an apostle."

"Okay." I replied, forcing him to be more specific. "How many churches have you started, or how many do you oversee?"

"I haven't started any churches," he said, "but I travel around giving apostolic counsel and direction to any church that I see needs it. I'm an apostolic father."

That did it for me! He couldn't point to a single thing to prove his apostolic authority. There were no churches, there was no following of people, nor were there any reputable ministers who could vouch for him. Unlike a true apostle, this man lacked the stamp of authenticity.

The seal of Paul's apostleship was the unarguable existence of the church in Corinth. He said, "You are the seal (or proof) of my apostleship" (1 Corinthians 9:2). Churches in other cities and regions were also the proof of Paul's apostleship. He had started many of them through his own evangelistic efforts and prophetic gifting, and had overseen their development with genuine apostolic anointing. As a wise master builder, he had laid their foundations, anchored active church bodies to them, and left each one in the care of capable leaders who yearned for his continuing support and oversight. The guy who came to me had none of that! All he had was an empty claim to apostolic authority and anointing. Genuine apostles don't have to tell people what they are. The mantles they wear speak for them. The Spirit of God bears witness with the hearts of the people to whom they reach, and other anointed ministers recognize them for what and who they really are.

When I first began learning about apostolic ministry, and how God was restoring it to the modern day Church, I was soon turned off by the heavy handedness I saw within several new streams. Many apostolic ministries in the 1970s and 80s were controlled by proud young men with a desire to add churches to their list like notches on a gun handle. They didn't care what they had to do push their agendas, or how badly they hurt people who didn't meet their criteria or who they considered to be a threat. And to attend some conferences was equally as offensive. Egotistical apostolic upstarts compared notes on how many churches they had either started or adopted. Spiritual pride was flagrant and rampant. Although there were many valid apostles emerging in those days, there were also many who lacked the anointing and grace to be what they claimed to be. If you compared them with some genuine apostolic men and women found in Asia, Africa, or South America, it was almost laughable.

But this is a new day. The apostolic pendulum, which swung too far into error in past years, has begun swinging back into proper position. Rather than tight-fisted control over their churches and ministers, apostles are seeing better results by networking with other apostolic streams, as well as by releasing the many gifted people under their own care. And rather than feel threatened by other powerful apostolic fathers, they are seeing the benefit of pulling together to reach the world for Christ.

The apostolic network we enjoy being part of in our region of North America's Appalachian Mountains, is called Appalachian Christian Outreach Ministries, International, or A.C.O.M.I. This stream provides us with a wonderful fellowship of churches and ministries that share a common vision for extending the kingdom throughout our eastern mountains. On a larger scale, we are united with White Horse Christian Center, an international apostolic network of churches and ministries that unites us with kingdom builders from across the nation and around the world. The one apostolic ministry does not cancel out the other, but the two work hand-in-hand to reach the world for Christ.

In the closing days of this age we will see many different apostolic ministries unite in an effort to win the world for Christ. There will be large teams and small ones, localized teams and more universal ones. Relationship will be the hallmark of these powerful ministries. Some major denominations will even begin abandoning old styles of church structure in favor of fresh new methods of governance through apostles and prophets and their anointed teams of people. It will be glorious!

6

His Good Hand of Blessing on Ezra

Some six decades after Zerubbabel led the first group of Jews back to Jerusalem to rebuild the temple, a scribe named Ezra, with the blessing of Persian king Artaxerxes, led a much smaller group of Jews (about 5,000) to Israel to restore the spiritual condition of the people. Although the temple had been restored, the hearts and lives of the Jews in that region were adrift. Without knowledge of the Word, and without an anointed teacher to unveil it, it was impossible for the people of God to get on target spiritually. Indeed, if the conduct of worshippers is not right, it matters not how beautiful the building in which they meet. Their edifice will be nothing more than a sepulcher full of dead men's bones.

Ezra, whose name means "Yahweh helps," was a priest, a scribe, and an expert in the Law of Moses (7:6, 11). The hand of the Lord was on him to bring restoration in a powerful way. Read these verses from Ezra, chapter seven, and note the recurring phrase concerning the hand of the Lord, which I have underlined:

This Ezra came up from Babylon; and he was a skilled scribe in the Law of Moses, which the Lord God of Israel had given. The king granted him all his request, <u>according to the hand of the Lord his God upon him.</u>
Vs. 6

On the first day of the first month he began his journey from Babylon, and on the first day of the fifth month he came to Jerusalem, <u>according to the good hand of his God upon him.</u> For Ezra had prepared his heart to seek the Law of the Lord, and to do it, and to teach statutes and ordinances in Israel.
Vs. 9-10

So I was encouraged, <u>as the hand of the Lord my God</u>

was upon me; and I gathered leading men of Israel to go up with me.

Vs. 28b

Several interesting ideas come to us from these verses, all relating to the fact that the hand of the Lord was upon Ezra's life and ministry.

First, Ezra *came up* from Babylon to Jerusalem, according to the good hand of his God upon him. Babylon means *confusion,* while Jerusalem means *city of peace.* Babylon was also a place of horrendous carnality, the kind of which has caused many lives to come to ruin. God's call on us is an *upward call,* demanding that we put forth an effort to reach for higher goals than what we settled for in the Babylon of our flesh. To walk in the flesh is to settle for life in the valley. To leave the valley for the heights with God is every believer's lifelong calling.

A friend recently visited our mountains from a distant city. One morning during his stay, he decided to climb the steep ridge behind my house and take in its fabulous view. With the rising sun quickly warming the morning, and the steep incline accelerating his metabolic rate, our friend was forced to peel off his jacket, sweater, and shirt. Although short of breath and overheated, he pushed himself up the side of that mountain. Finally he reached the top of the ridge and collapsed in a heap, struggling to catch his breath. After a moment he stood and turned to view one of the most beautiful vistas in the State of Virginia. Stretching far to the north, the celebrated Blue Grass Valley rolled along, culminating at the foot of Snowy Mountain, nearly thirty miles away. Not far to the south, the beautiful valley melted into the rugged ridges and hidden hollows of an isolated area known as Little Egypt. As he stood, somewhat mesmerized by the grandeur of our beautiful region, the Spirit of God whispered these strong words to his heart: "The higher you go in Me the better the view will be, but it will cost you something to get there." These words reverberated throughout his being as he knelt down to consider the challenge God was placing before him. Would he descend the ridge and return to life as usual, seeking to tread, as so many others, the path of least resistance? Or would he take the harder course, press on, and lay hold of that for which Christ Jesus had also laid hold of him?

Beloved, each of us has a choice to make in life. We can decide to stay in the valleys of carnality where nothing much is required of us, and where nothing exciting ever happens, or we can force our flesh up the side of the mountain and into the heights with God. It would have been easier to stay in Babylon under moderate Persian control, but Ezra knew he had to follow Heaven's leading into an awesome destiny. Sure there would be an arduous journey through hostile territory, and sure there would be opposition from hateful adversaries once he arrived in Jerusalem to commence his important work. But Ezra also believed that all of these struggles would be worth it in the end. Ezra's choice to ascend into his destiny brought God's hand upon him in wonderful ways.

The second thing to note concerning Ezra is that he was a *skilled* scribe, an expert when understanding and applying the Law of God. This was so only because he had prepared his heart to seek the Law of the Lord at personal cost to himself. In his youth, while other young men spent hours in frivolous activities, Ezra had pored over the Scriptures, equipping himself for the destiny God had for him. When the Lord sees such a level of devotion on someone, He is pleased to place both his *good hand* and strong mantle of anointing on his shoulders.

Thirdly, when one develops his skill, he gains favor with important people who can help him accomplish his mission. King Artaxerxes "granted [Ezra] all his request, according to the hand of the Lord his God upon him." In many cases, the hand of the

Lord creates the favor we need with important men. A verse in Proverbs also applies here: "A man's gift makes room for him, and brings him before great men" (18:16). Because Ezra was faithful to recognize and polish his talents, the Lord made him noticeable to powerful people who could help him complete his assignment. If you are gifted in certain areas, but never take the pains to develop those gifts, important people will continually overlook you as they search for those who have faithfully developed their talents. Why aren't you used more? Why has the pastor not noticed or used your gifts? Why can't the apostle see you as valuable to his mission to extend the kingdom? Perhaps because you have been wasting your time and energy on things that mean nothing to the Lord. Your time would be better served if you would recognize your inborn aptitudes and apply your energies to making them the best that they can be for His glory. Perhaps your very character has remained unshaped for lack of quality time with God in prayer, fasting and worship.

Those of us in Spirit-filled circles have all known young Christians who received powerful prophecies concerning their ministries. With great excitement they have shared all that the prophets told them about their future. However, as the months passed, we watched as these youngsters returned to spending time and energy pursuing hobbies and amusements that failed to prepare them for the fulfillment of prophetic destinies. Although many of them possessed the raw talent to become effective warriors for God, they neither developed those talents nor polished their skills so that God could use them for His purposes. As a result, their prophecies remained unborn.

Fourthly, when one is faithful to develop inborn skills for God's glory, he moves steadily from a state of confusion and aimlessness in spiritual things to a profound sense of purpose and fulfillment.[4] This person's life is filled with what I call "faith projects," those wonderful spiritual activities that are richly rewarding and fulfilling. But alas, because many Christians are not settled in their callings, there is always an ample supply of complainers around.

Because they never have a sense of where they are going or where they belong, they are never content with life as it is. Rather than making the most of where they are, they miss what God wants them to do. Instead, they sit around pouting and making other people as miserable as they are.

The fifth thing I would like to point out is that it took Ezra and his entourage four months to travel from Babylon to Jerusalem, from confusion to peace. Four is the number for transition. When the good hand of God is upon us, garnering the favor of important men and bringing us from confusion to peace, the transition requires some time. Therefore, we mustn't be discouraged by the journey, no matter how long it takes, nor how arduous it seems to be. Pilgrims remember that they are on a journey, and so develop the force of perseverance as they trod through this world's wastelands. They know a City awaits them, and do not lose heart as they sojourn in anticipation of coming glory. In their hearts "are the highways to Zion" (Psalm 84:5, NAS), and so they press ahead.

Sixthly, Ezra was *encouraged* as the hand of the Lord was upon him. Nothing but the hand of God can encourage us when we are carrying out an important work. We are never adequate in and of ourselves to accomplish anything for God, but when we know our adequacy is from Him, we can press through with confidence and complete the task.

When God instructed me to begin a teaching ministry in my hometown—a community where everyone knew me and could easily remember my pre-conversion days of intemperance—I felt totally unqualified for the job. To my thinking an official man with credentials conferred upon him by a prestigious seminary would better accomplish what God was leading me to do. But the Lord chose me, and I was obliged to respond. It has been many years since I began the Bible study in my home that grew into a church and international ministry, and I gratefully give credit to the Lord for encouraging me along the way. Although the journey from that meager beginning to where we are today has been fraught with many frustrations and setbacks, the support given by the hand of

God has been even more undeniable and abundant. Ezra was encouraged *as the hand of the Lord was upon him.*

The seventh and final point I'd like to emphasize concerning Ezra's work in Israel is how he, like Zerubbabel before him, was able to gather *leading men* to go up with him to Jerusalem. When one is making the climb from Babylon to Jerusalem, from a state of exile and confusion to one of purposeful labor and progress, it helps to have the right people on the team. These are men and women with a certain daring about them, people who are willing to take risks and pioneer new things under the right leadership and guidance. These are people who recognize a leader's unique assignment and sense a strong call to support him in its fulfillment.

In chapter eight, Ezra recorded, "Then, *by the good hand of our God upon us,* they brought us a man of understanding" (vs. 18). That man was Sherebiah, whose name means, "flame of the Lord." Certainly this man carried a fervency and zeal that shone brightly, warming many with whom he was in covenant relationship. At other times, however, his flame might have been used to singe adversaries who opposed the Lord's work. It is certain that Sherebiah knew the difference, as he was a "man of understanding." A flame burning bright and hot must be accompanied by wisdom in order to be most effective. Wild fires can bring about much death and destruction, but controlled fires can produce much warmth and comfort. When a believer is full of misguided and undisciplined zeal, he is like a wild fire, doing more damage than good. When this occurs, the Lord must allow his fire to be extinguished by the waters of disappointment. Humility coupled with great zeal is what the Lord is after in each believer, and until the arrogance and pride that ride the drafts of spiritual fire are dealt with, the Lord will not use us very much.

Sharpen the Ax

If the ax is dull, and one does not sharpen the edge,
then he must use more strength; but wisdom brings success.
Ecclesiastes 10:10

Believers with misguided and undisciplined zeal are also like the users of dull axes who try to fell great trees. Their axes may sparkle in the sunshine, and even be affixed to solid hickory handles, but if the edges are dull, and they don't have the wisdom to make every stroke count, a ridiculous amount of strength and time will be required to bring the trees to the ground. "But wisdom brings success," or as the King James Version puts it, "wisdom is profitable to direct." A sharpened axe, wielded by a wise and experienced axe man, will topple a tree in less than half the time it takes an overly zealous novice who swings a dull axe without knowing how to direct his strokes. Indeed, the novice with a dull axe is much more dangerous to himself and others than any twenty experienced men who use a sharp axe with wisdom and skill. Dull axes tend to bounce off their targets and ricochet in any direction, where sharp axes cut deep and true. Sherebiah was like a well-controlled flame, but he was also like a wise man taking big bites out of a tree with each skillfully directed stroke of his sharpened ax. As a member of Ezra's team, sent to restore proper worship in Israel, Sheribiah's wisdom was priceless. How valuable are you to your leaders? Are you an out-of-control flame? Perhaps you are a dull and misguided axe. Always be willing to submit your plans and dreams to legitimate spiritual authorities for their wisdom and guidance.

Ezra had other significant men on the team, and each of them had a peculiar role to play in the overall plan of God. By examining the meaning of their names, we can gather a better understanding of the various strengths God desired to spread among the men who went up to Jerusalem with Ezra. There was

65

Hashabiah, whose name means, "regarded by Jehovah." It is always wonderful to be linked to a person whom God regards highly. Favor seems to drop around them like dew on the morning grass. Jeshaiah was also united with Ezra. His name means "deliverance of Jehovah." Whenever a great work is underway, it is good to have Jehovah's delivering power on hand. That power seems to manifest through certain individuals more than others, and if they are on your team, you are blessed indeed.

For a listing of other men who served Ezra, as well as the meanings of their names, see endnotes.[5] This collection of gifted men were used to restore proper order to culture and worship in Israel. Their very names bespeak qualities every spiritual team should covet. Only the hand of the Lord can gather such reliable and gifted servants together. If a leader attempts to gather them by manipulation, coercion or deceit, their hearts will never truly become united to his, and frustration and failure will be the inevitable result.

Years earlier, David expressed his own understanding of this important truth, and praised God for being the One, "Who subdues my people under me" (Psalm 144:2). David never lacked the service of good men, and he knew to give God the credit for all they accomplished together. Indeed, when God's good hand is upon His leaders, whether they are in high places of authority, or in humble stations of life, the provision of wonderful people is released.

Seeking God is Imperative

Ezra ended his comments about the hand of the Lord by saying, *"The hand of our God is upon all those for good who seek Him,* but His power and wrath are against all those who forsake Him"* (8:22).

I once heard Derek Prince comment: "The difference between seeking the Lord and a prayer meeting is this: When you finish a prayer meeting you quit, but when you seek God you don't quit till you find Him." Ezra understood this vital truth, and devoted his life to its practice. Seeking the Lord involves the combination of three essential practices. First, we must *inquire* of the Lord, seeking His counsel. We then must *listen* for His still small voice. And third, we must *be willing to wait* for the Lord, realizing that His timing is often different from ours. He may speak the moment we ask, or He may wait before speaking and revealing His counsel to us. When this happens we must be persistent. His delay may simply be His way of seeing just how badly we want His blessing.

Refusing to Let Go

When Jacob wrestled the Man beside the ford of Jabbok, which means, "a pouring out," he had to wrestle until it cost him something valuable. In his case, it was a healthy hip, representing reliance on his own wit, cunning, agility, and knack for extracting himself from difficult and trying situations. Prior to this time, Jacob was a supplanter and heel-grabber, a shrewd and conniving man. At the ford of Jabbok he had to offer up these self-serving qualities so that God might pour in His own acceptable ones. Sometimes we have to pour ourselves out, that God might pour Himself in!

As he wrestled with the Lord, Jacob had to use every fiber of his being. As a sport, wrestling involves the commitment of the whole man. One's mind, will and strength must be totally involved, or defeat is certain! In the Hebrew, the word *wrestle* literally means, "to take hold with an encircling grasp." Rather than attempt to pin the Lord's shoulder blades to the ground, Jacob wrapped his arms and legs around God and would not be pried away! As dawn approached, the Lord said, "Let me go, for the day breaks!" But Jacob would not release Him. This tells us something very significant. It tells us that the Lord has a weak spot, a place where He is vulnerable. Think of it. The God of creation has a soft place, and you can touch it. And what is this soft spot? Where can a man prevail with God? The answer is simple: Yahweh cannot free

Himself from one whose heart earnestly seeks Him. The God of wonders beyond our galaxy cannot pry Himself loose from one who clings to Him with all of his heart, soul, mind and strength!

Through the dark night of the soul and until the break of day, Jacob wrestled, pouring out his heart to the Lord. When night finally lifted, and the new day dawned, the inner enemies of pride, fear, and conniving (the impulses that made Jacob trust in himself and not God) were eradicated, and he walked with a limp of humility and brokenness. He had successfully wrestled with the Lord, declaring, "I will not let you go unless you bless me!" Jacob's unyielding determination caused him to prevail, not against a reluctance to bless him on God's part, but by impressing God with his desire to be blessed. Never is there a reluctance on the Lord's part to bless—He wants to bless us, but He does want to see how badly we want the blessing!

After prevailing with God and men (for when we have prevailed with God, we will prevail with men), Jacob received a new name (Israel), and was enabled to *cross over* Peniel, which means "the face of God." This speaks of securing a place in the light of His countenance. As this man, now named Israel, crossed over Peniel, the sun (Son) rose upon him, shining down warming rays to invigorate and embolden him to seize his destiny. Like, Israel, we must take hold of God with an encircling grasp "until the day dawns, and the morning star rises in [our] hearts" (2 Peter 1:19).

The King James Version says: "But as a prince hast thou power with God and with men, and hast prevailed" (vs. 28). This is very significant for those who want to impact others with the gospel, for when one truly prevails with God in prayer, he gains more power with those he longs to lead in the way of righteousness. Indeed, when a man's ways please the Lord, He can make even his enemies to be at peace with him. When Esau started out to meet Jacob with 400 men, very possibly 400 battle-ready men, a bloodbath may have been on his mind. But on the lonely night when Jacob prevailed with God in prayer, Esau experienced a change of heart and was ready to meet his brother in a spirit of peace and reconciliation.

How vigorously will you wrestle with God tonight? To what ends will you go in order to cross over [before] His face and win the hearts of those who consider you an enemy?

A Summary of Chapter Six

As we close chapter six, let us recapitulate a few key points showing how God's hand was on Ezra, and how we too can benefit from this blessing.

1. The hand of the Lord is the agent by which God lifts His people from the depths of confusion to a place of peace, security and purpose. The hand of God brought Ezra up from Babylon, meaning "confusion," to Jerusalem, meaning "city of peace." God can do the same for us if we will offer our lives to Him.

2. To walk with clear insight and miraculous power, one must propel himself out of the self-imprisoning valleys of carnality and into the heights with God. At higher levels of communion with the Lord, fresh baptisms of power and wisdom are gained to make us victorious over all the works of the Devil.

3. Preparation for effectiveness is so very important. As Ezra readied his heart by filling it with God's Word, his inborn skills were enhanced and heightened, and a greater anointing came to him from the hand of the Lord. Tremendous devotion is required if one will be used mightily in a ministry of restoration!

4. Skills and talents that are regularly exercised and developed will open doors that otherwise would remain closed. The hand of the Lord honored Ezra by winning for him the favor of king Artaxerxes. God's hand gives us esteem with important people when we are seeking to walk in His plan for our lives.

5. The hand of the Lord also brings us encouragement when the battle is raging. Without His encouragement, we would lose heart and give up the fight. Ezra said, "So I was encouraged as the hand of the Lord my God was upon me" (7:28).

6. Evidence of God's hand being upon one who is called to restore something to God's people will be an ample supply of willing and gifted helpers. Without God's favorable hand in this regard, the servant will experience continual frustration as he tries to convince people to help him, or attempts to accomplish great things by himself.

7. Godly wisdom is the stone that sharpens the ax of zeal and enthusiasm. Without wisdom's sharpening effect, zeal can be a misguided and dangerous instrument, bringing much damage to those who get too close to it.

8. Seeking the Lord, and not simply attending a prayer meeting, is essential if we will see the fulfillment of His purposes in our lives and ministries. As we saw, the difference between seeking the Lord and attending a prayer meeting is this: When you complete a prayer meeting you quit. When you are seeking the Lord, you don't quit until you find Him.

7
His Determined Hand on Nehemiah

Few stories in Scripture thrill me more than Nehemiah's. His keen interest in the welfare of Jerusalem and its inhabitants is gripping. Although he was comfortable and secure as cupbearer to king Artaxerxes in Shushan, the citadel of the Persian Empire, he was deeply saddened to learn that all was not well in Jerusalem, and that Ezra's work of restoring proper worship in Israel was hampered because no protective walls surrounded the Holy City.

Without regard to his own welfare, Nehemiah boldly returned to his homeland to challenge his countrymen to rise up and rebuild the shattered wall of Jerusalem. Ezra the scribe had done a masterful job envisioning many Jews in Israel, but without a protective wall around the city, they were vulnerable to the desires of their many enemies. Bold, witty and industrious, Nehemiah arrived just in time, complete with the blessing of the Persian king, and the courage to see the project through to the end.

The Lord looks for such men and women today, servants who are not afraid to face the wrath of angry demons as they build up the kingdom of God in hostile lands. Nehemiah faced opposition from within, without, and everywhere round about, but he wouldn't quit!

Sir Winston Churchill once asked the question: "How is it that the ship, battered by the waves, can make progress, though it is one and the waves are so many?" His answer was simple yet profound. "Because the ship has purpose." Nehemiah also had purpose. He had to have it, because the opposition against him was intense and relentless.

His first opposition came in the form of vicious ridicule and scorn (Nehemiah 2:19). Sanballat, Tobiah and Geshem, three despicable agents of Satan, accused him of rebelling against the very king who had sanctioned his mission. Sounds like the Devil, doesn't it? As the accuser of the brethren, he never ceases to question our calling and make us feel like God is no longer for us. By this he hopes to confuse us and cause our hearts to faint. Consistent prayer is our only safeguard against his plan. Jesus said, "Men ought always to pray, and not faint" (Luke 18:1).

The second opposition raised against Nehemiah came in the form of indignant and caustic mockery. Sanballat, whose Babylonian name means, "Sin has given life," was a true scoundrel. In his name's meaning, *Sin* was the Babylonian moon-god. But the full meaning of Sanballat's name—*Sin has given life*—applies accurately to the vitality his nature gave to the opposition raised against Nehemiah. This human devil battered the work mercilessly, asking sarcastic questions like: "What are these feeble Jews doing? Will they fortify themselves? Will they offer sacrifices? Will they complete it in a day? Will they revive the stones from the heaps of rubbish?" Sanballat had more questions than there were answers for. But Nehemiah knew not to waste time answering his critics. As Christians we should avoid this snare as well. It is impossible to defend yourself and reveal the nature of Jesus at the same time.

Sanballat's third opposition was the threat of physical violence (4:7). As Nehemiah began to shut off the gaps and breaches in the wall, the enemy became very angry. Satan always hates it when we begin shutting off his entrances to our lives, and will, therefore, increase his persecution against us.

How Nehemiah Succeeded

Nehemiah endured at least three more attempts to stop him from rebuilding the wall around Jerusalem, but he would not succumb to even one of them. He faced and handled inner friction among the ranks (5:1); denied a cordial but deceptive invitation to what would have been a harmful conclave with his enemies (6:2); and resisted the Devil's relentless effort to instill the fear of failure in his builders (5:9). Nehemiah's responses were God-honoring and foolproof. In the face of every form of opposition, he prayed. "Nevertheless we made our prayer to God" (4:9).

Not only did this Old Testament apostle pray, but also he held fast to the promise of God by confession (2:20). Not only did he confess the promises, but also he surrounded himself with good people—people who had a mind to work (4:6). Not only did he surround himself with good people, but he also positioned those people in strategic places along the wall (4:13). It is one thing to have good people; it is another to know how to position them so that they can be most effective. Not only did Nehemiah place his people correctly, but he also encouraged them to "Remember the Lord, great and awesome" (4:14). He inspired them by reminding them that they were building and fighting, not simply for themselves, but also for their brethren, sons, daughters, wives and houses (4:14). He was generational in his thinking, and not like Hezekiah who, in his day, only showed concern for his own generation. When faced with the future demise of his people, Hezekiah was relieved that he, at least, would have peace in his own day. (See 2 Kings 20:16-19.) Few things should inspire people more than an understanding that the safety and success of their descendants depends largely on what they do today.

Across the world today there are those who believe the armed forces of free nations should pull out of places where they are making a stand against tyranny and terrorism. They entertain the idea that if we will only stop resisting the terrorists, they will somehow let us live in peace. They hold to the notion that appeasement is a better course than armed resistance. Respectfully, I disagree. According to Sir Winston Churchill, "Appeasement is like feeding a crocodile, hoping you'll be the last one he eats." In other words, the appeaser says, "If we just feed the beast what it wants, it will remain happy and leave us alone." But I say, "Don't count on it!" When an enemy like Islamic terrorism shows its evil hand as it did on September 11, 2001, in New York City, as well as on hundreds of days since then, we dare not stick our heads in the sand! In a perfect world we will live at peace with all men, but until Jesus returns to establish that perfect world, thugs and murderers will continue to covet power and raise a serious threat to everyone on earth. Therefore duly authorized magistrates and their governments must resist them!

The despicable nature of the unsaved human heart leans heavily toward the exploitation of weak and defenseless people. God knew this when He endorsed justifiable force to restrain evil. Until Jesus returns, evil men will seek to dominate the weak, and therefore must be withstood by God-sanctioned authorities. Indeed, the Lord of armies sanctions the governments of benevolent nations to put down the threats of malevolent ones (Romans 13:1-4). Even if few governments have the nerve to stand against evil aggression, a few nations always will. God's word declares that when proper authorities execute wrath on evildoers, they "do not bear the sword in vain." The police and military forces of any nation have the right, as well as the God-ordained responsibility, to protect their citizens from the aggressive hand of tyranny. American general, George C. Marshall, Chairman of the Joint Chiefs of Staff during World War Two, made this timeless statement concerning the subject we are considering:

We have tried since the birth of our nation to promote our love of peace by a display of weakness. This course has cost us millions of lives and billions of treasure. The reasons are quite understandable: The world does not seriously regard the desires of the weak. Weakness presents too great a temptation to the strong. We must, if we are to realize the hopes we may now dare for a lasting peace, reinforce our will for peace with strength. We must make it clear to the potential gangsters of the world that if they dare break our peace they will do so at their great peril!

While we should never have a lust for war, neither should we be neglectful of our descendant's right to live free from the dominion of devils, villains and thugs. Even Nehemiah, at God's direction, placed weapons in the hands of his builders, along with trowels (4:13-17). After making their prayers to God (4:9), they set a watch against the terrorists who wished to come upon them and destroy what they were doing for God's glory.

Nehemiah also insisted his people listen for the sound of the trumpet, and respond to the call to rally together whenever it sounded night or day (4:20). He understood that builder/warriors must respond quickly to the signals sent by their leaders. The Church today fails in many arenas of spiritual warfare because of the rebellious and independent attitude displayed by many of God's people. Many spiritual leaders mourn the fact that so few people respond when a fast is proclaimed, or show up when a prayer meeting is convened. People will eagerly gather at conferences where the power is flowing to heal and prosper them, but they will not join their own people to pray and lay hold of God in deep corporate intercession. The call to rally and fight in prayer and spiritual warfare must be heard and followed *if* the last days Church will accomplish the end time mission God has given it.

Nehemiah also exercised strong, impartial leadership when injustice pervaded his people (5:1-12). Regardless of who a person was, the great wall builder required integrity. He even went so far as to bind the nobles and rulers to a curse if they refused to make things right with their brethren: "Then I shook out the fold of my garment and said, 'So may God shake out each man from his house and property, who does not perform this promise. Even thus may he be shaken out and emptied'" (5:13).

Because he feared God, Nehemiah also refused to treat himself with special privileges—privileges that were within the scope of his authority (5:14-18). Like any great leader, he sought to set an example before his people, an example of modesty, humility and contentment with what God had provided. The leader who lives *above* his people rarely wins the affection of those people.

In the classic military manual, *The Art of War,* famed oriental general, Sun Tzu wrote:

Regard your soldiers as your children, and they will follow you into the deepest valleys; look on them as your beloved sons, and they will stand by you even unto death.[6]

The brilliant general went on to relate the story of how another famous general named Wu Ch'i treated his own warriors:

He wore the same clothes and ate the same food as the meanest of his soldiers, refused to have either a horse to ride or a mat to sleep on, carried his own surplus rations wrapped in a parcel, and shared every hardship with his men. When one of his soldiers was suffering from an abscess, Wu Ch'i himself sucked out the virus. The soldier's mother, hearing this, began wailing and lamenting. Somebody asked her, "Why do you cry? Your son is only a common soldier, and yet the commander-in-chief himself has sucked the poison from his sore." The woman replied: "Many years ago, Lord Wu performed a similar service for my husband, who never left him afterward, and finally met his death at the hands of the enemy. And now that he has done the same for my son, he too will fall fighting I know not where!"

Nehemiah, although a stern and focused leader, never exalted himself above those with whom the Lord had called him to serve. His workers recognized and appreciated this, and remained loyal to him for the remainder of their lives.

Not only was Nehemiah a humble and generous leader, but also he was a single-minded man, determined to complete his mission regardless of whom it angered. When his enemies feigned friendliness, the wise builder refused to come down from the wall and waste time talking with them. He knew their true nature had not changed, and so wouldn't give them the time of day (6:1-4).

An Anointed Team of Builders

As an apostolic type, Nehemiah surveyed Jerusalem's crumbled wall by night, with only a few men at his side (2:12). He did not depend on the approval of the whole Church, but the approval of the One who called him. The anointed builder well understood that the kingdom of God is not a democracy, but a theocracy, with power descending down from God, not rising up from beneath. One sure way to destroy a God-ordained work, even before it is finished, is to ask all the people how they think things should be done. If you do, you'll get forty different opinions, and confusion will be the terrible result. Nehemiah alone had the call, the gifting, and the anointing to oversee and direct the great project in Jerusalem. Yet like Zerubbabel and Ezra before him, he knew to surround himself with a wise team of people. He cherished the counsel of those with an ear tuned to Heaven. Their names were loaded with meaning, indicating the strengths and talents the Lord had in mind for so great a work.[7]

As we read the remarkable account of how Nehemiah built the wall around the Holy City in just fifty-two days, we realize that the hand of God on His servant could only have accomplished this. In fact, two verses actually credit the Lord's good hand as being that which initiated and enabled the completion of the work through this anointed team of builders. (See Nehemiah 2:8 and 18.)

Beloved, in this day of restoration, let us covet the hand of the Lord as Nehemiah did. Only by God's wisdom, anointing and favor, will we be able to accomplish His will on earth, and hasten days of great revival and a genuine return to New Testament power.

8
The Glory of the Latter House

Religion has become formal and empty, simply going through the motions, but out of touch with spiritual reality. Religious leaders, by their rejection of God's word and standards, are stumbling, and making people stumble too. Humanistic philosophy—man trusting in man for answers—prevails. No longer are there any absolutes. Good is called evil and evil, good.

- Arthur Wallis

In the 1980s, Wallis' book, *The Radical Christian,* called believers to the same all-or-nothing commitment to Christ that characterized the early Church. The call is as strong today as it was then. If our religion will once again become full and vigorous, properly representing the God of the Bible and impacting the nations, then we must have a restoration to radicalism.

When one restores a piece of furniture, he strips away the dried, hardened layers of all that has covered the original luster. Until he has discovered and penetrated the earliest coating, and created a sheen identical to the one formed by its maker, he has not truly restored the piece. We live in a day when the world desperately needs to see the Church's original sheen. The world must see the government, the power and the glory of genuine Christianity before it will embrace the Son of Man. Praise God! That revelation is coming forth!

Have You Heard the Lion Roar?

Have you heard the lion roar? Peter had, and Jesus told him how it happened.

"Who do men say that I, the Son of Man, am?"

"You are the Christ, the Son of the living God!" replied Peter.

"Blessed are you, Simon Bar-Jonah," Jesus responded, "for flesh and blood has not revealed this to you, but My Father who is in heaven!"

By revelation of the Holy Spirit, Peter had come to realize that Jesus was the long-awaited Messiah. The name *Simon Bar-Jonah* literally means, "Hearing, Son of Dove." Deep in his spirit-man, Peter had heard the voice of the Dove, saying, "Jesus is Messiah." The Lord went on to explain that upon this rock of revelation, the Church would be built, and the gates of Hades would not prevail against it!

When a revelation of who Jesus is comes to any man, *and he receives it*, to him it becomes a rock! God can do little in a person's life if eternal truth doesn't become revelation deep within his heart!

Mental information is not enough. Although information is good, it alone cannot save you. Information must drop the eighteen inches to your heart and become spiritual revelation for it to do any good. Revelation is spiritual, and can set the stage for awesome things to happen!

It wasn't until my heart received a revelation of Jesus as Savior, that I was saved.

It wasn't until my heart received a revelation of Jesus as Healer, that I was healed.

It wasn't until my heart received a revelation of Jesus as mighty Creator, that I began to truly reverence Him.

When Does the Lion Roar?

Surely the Lord God does nothing, unless He reveals His secret to His servants the prophets. A lion has roared!

Who will not fear? The Lord God has spoken! Who can but prophesy?   Amos 3:7-8

The Biblical principle that is seen in these verses is thrilling! It says that God will do *nothing* unless revelation enters into the heart of a man. Look at this truth:

The Lord God will do nothing unless He reveals!

When revelation comes to a man from the Holy Spirit, he hears the Lion roar! Abstract things become concrete. Hazy ideas and notions become tangible and fixed; his heart becomes steadfast and established (Psalm 112:7-8). When one hears the Lion roar, imparted revelation begins to burn in his bones, and he cannot keep it to himself (Jeremiah 20:9). When one hears the Lion roar, the life in the revelation becomes like new wine in a wineskin that has no vent. The person must open his lips and speak, or he will explode! (See Job 32:18-20.) *"The Lord has spoken!"* Amos said. *"Who can but prophesy?"*

Peter had heard the Lion roar, and was able to comprehend the significance of the Son of Man! Many spiritual patriarchs before him had also heard the Lion roar, and had gone on to accomplish marvelous things for the Lord.

Beloved, have you heard the Lion roar? Every time the *logos* word becomes *rhema* in your heart, you hear the Lion roar! Every time a revelation finds a place deep inside your spirit man, you hear the Lion roar! And only after you have heard His roar, concerning any given subject, can you overpower the gates of Hell that stand before your life! Therefore, spend more time with God in prayer, more time with Him in the Word, and listen for the Lion to roar! His roar will fill you with courage to do the impossible and achieve the outrageous! His roar will strike fear in the hearts of your enemies.

Receiving the Revelation

The Lion of the Tribe of Judah—even Jesus—is presently roaring in the ears of many people. But unless they receive His roar by faith, it will do them no good.

When Ezekiel received revelation of the Lord, and actually saw Him in His glorious power, he fell on his face, overwhelmed by His presence (Ezekiel 1:28; 3:23).

When Daniel saw the Lord, he fell into a deep sleep *on his face* (Daniel 10:9). He was overwhelmed by His presence.

When John saw the Lord in His radiant glory; he "fell at His feet as dead," overwhelmed by His presence; overwhelmed by the revelation of His Deity (Revelation 1:17).

Notice how each man fell *forward* when he received a revelation of Jesus. The same principle will hold true for you and me today. We will literally "fall forward" in life if we will receive the revelation of Christ when it comes. But right on the other hand, we will "fall backwards" in life if we reject revelation when it comes.

On the evening the temple guards came to arrest Jesus in the Garden of Gethsemane, He revealed Himself as God by saying "I Am!" (See John 18:4-6.) At this bold declaration, the soldiers all "drew back and fell to the ground." I maintain that they fell the wrong way; they fell backwards in life because they did not receive the revelation of who this Man was.

Courageous Last Days People

Only those who have heard the Lion's roar will accomplish important things in the kingdom in coming days; only those who have heard His roar will be prepared to do unpopular things and defy the clamor of gutless and comfortable people. Only men and women who have prophetic revelation will be courageous enough to restore things in the last days. Courage is not the absence of fear in crisis situations, but is the quality of spirit that enables us to face down our

82

foes, defeat the indomitable, scale the insurmountable, and achieve the impossible—or die trying! Without prophetic revelation burning in the heart, people with good intentions back down when the fight gets nasty. Revelation holds a man steady under pressure. Revelation keeps him calm when adversity raises its ugly head. Jesus went all the way to Calvary because of a revelation in His heart. He knew who He was, and what His mission was to accomplish. Revelation made Him courageous enough to complete God's will!

Courage attracts the Holy Spirit just as fear attracts the demons! When the Holy Spirit responds to courage, He adds His own wisdom and mettle to the equation, making it possible for us to know and do what otherwise would be impossible.

Courage is required if we will cross over into a meaningful future and take ground for God. If the Church will probe her original luster, and bring manifest victory to this dying world, then individuals and groups alike must again become people of courage!

Items Being Restored

Much of what the Church has lacked for centuries is in the process of being restored for the final harvest. Some things are well on their way to final restoration, while other things are just now coming forth.

When the Jews in Zerubbabel's day began rebuilding the temple, the prophet Haggai encouraged them by promising that the glory of the latter house would be greater than that of the former house (Haggai 2:9). It is very likely that the Jews who heard him believed they were building a house that would outshine Solomon's temple in splendor and glory. But it never did. Yet without a full understanding of its significance, Haggai made his declaration. It is obvious to us today that the prophet was declaring a time far beyond his own, when the glory of God would rise upon a *spiritual* temple God would call the Church of Jesus Christ.

He prophesied a time when millions of Jesus men and women would encompass the globe with a Holy Spirit baptism to preach the glorious gospel in preparation for the end of the age. The glory on *this* house would indeed exceed anything that had been seen before. Haggai's prophecy also pointed to the day when Messiah Himself would take up His throne, Jerusalem, and the peoples of the nations would flow together to worship Him there. (See Micah 4:1-5.)

Today, God is in the process of beautifying and adorning His spiritual temple. He is taking the Church from glory to glory, from strength to strength, and from faith to faith. Indeed, as "the path of the righteous is like the first gleam of dawn, shining ever brighter till the full light of day" (Proverbs 4:18), so the true Church is increasing and reflecting God's glory amidst the final dark years of this age. As time rolls on, and the darkness intensifies, the glory rising on the Church will dispel the night and burn away the fog. We will see things more clearly as time advances. As the sun rises higher in these last days, things hidden in darkness will come to the light, and truths long covered by the dust of time and tradition will be uncovered to our great advantage.

In the last few centuries, pivotal truths and practices which needed to be restored have been embraced by the Church. They are:

1. Revelation concerning the priesthood of every believer, as well as a knowledge that the just shall live by faith (1500s.)

2. The translation of Scripture into the common language of man. (1500s to 1600s.)

3. A revelation that salvation is a free gift received by repentance and faith. (1500s—1700s.)

4. Large open-air meetings to reach the lost. Revivalist era preachers like Whitfield, Wesley, Asbury, Finney and Moody. (1730s to present day.)

5. Large public prayer meetings, followed by sweeping seasons of revival and awakening. —Fulton Street prayer meeting and prayer revival, which spread to the nations. (1858 to early 1860s.)

6. Emphasis on world missions. (1700s to present day.)

7. The Pentecostal Revival. (Late 1800s to present day.)

8. The healing revivals. (Early and middle 1900s to present day.)

9. The charismatic renewal in mainline churches. (1960s and 1970s.)

10. World evangelism. —Major radio and television outreaches, and massive overseas crusades. (1960s thru the present day.)

11. The teaching of faith, healing and the authority of the believer. (Throughout the 1900s and into the 2000s.)

12. Major restoration of the teaching ministry. (1960s and into the present.)

13. Restoration of spiritual warfare and demonology doctrine. (1970s and into the present.)

14. Restoration of prophetic praise and worship; the restoration of the tabernacle of David. —Maranatha

Music, Integrity Hosanna, Vineyard, Hillsong, and many more. (1970s-2000s.)

15. Restoration of New Testament forms of church government, and the recovery of the five-fold ministry gifts. Many major and minor apostolic networks birthed worldwide. (1970s-2000s.)

16. Restored appreciation of Jewish roots by the New Testament Church. (1980s-2000s.)

17. Restoration of the prophetic gifts and offices. (1970s-2000s.)

18. Restoration of and re-emphasis on intercessory prayer ministry for revival and awakening. (1980s-2000s.)

19. Renewed emphasis on the River and Glory of God. (1990s-2000s.)

20. Restoration of governmental intercession, prayer that directly impacts governments and their people. (2000s.)

A Davidic Anointing

The blessed anointing once released on David of Israel, is also being released on a Davidic-style people being raised up today. Israel's greatest king was also a man after God's own heart, and such people today are tapping into an anointing much like the one he carried. In this anointing, things lost are being restored to God's people, and the kingdom increase this king enjoyed in his day is occurring in our day as well. If the tabernacle of David is truly being restored in our day and hour, as Amos 9:11 prophesied it would be, then all other aspects of David's anointing are also being restored. Let us examine what Ethan wrote concerning this special anointing.

*I have found My servant David; with My holy oil I
have anointed him, <u>with whom My hand shall be established</u>...*
Psalm 89:20-21

Part and parcel of the restoration process occurring today is the type of anointing David carried as God-appointed king of Israel. It was an anointing for the wilderness, an anointing for warfare, and an anointing for reigning. The fact that God's hand established him in all three aspects is significant. Whether he was unknown or well known, surviving the brutality of the wilderness or enjoying the plush surroundings of the palace, David was blessed with unction from the Holy Spirit that commanded his ultimate success. Truly, God's hand was upon him.

Ethan continued his statement by revealing the blessings of the Davidic anointing:

My arm shall strengthen him. The enemy shall not outwit him, nor the son of wickedness afflict him. I will beat down his foes before his face, and plague those who hate him. But My faithfulness and My mercy shall be with him, and in My name his horn shall be exalted.
Vs. 21b-24

The end time battles confronting God's people will reveal the blessings we read about here. In YAH alone will be our everlasting strength (Isaiah 26:3), and with the same Spirit that was on David, we will score victories that would have been lost at any other time in history. This will happen because of the combination of two powerful dynamics: One, we are at the time the Bible calls "the end," and two, we are a generation of believers consumed with a vision for revival and awakening that hasn't been seen for decades! These two dynamics produce a powerful mix, one that is lethal for the kingdom of darkness, but glorious for the purposes of God!

A cleverness that far exceeds that of our enemies will also carry the Church through coming days. The enemy will not outwit us! This spiritual cunning will work to protect and preserve the Church, and the strong hand of the Lord will deal firmly with those who oppose His agenda. At the same time, God's faithfulness and mercy shall establish His people on every island and continent as they proclaim His truth to the nations! The rising tide of signs, wonders and miracles will be awesome to behold in coming days, and multiplied millions of people will be given the opportunity to receive the Lord who makes bare His holy arm before the nations.

In some nations, it is unlawful to convert people by telling them they need to repent and accept the Lord Jesus. It is an even greater crime to challenge their national religion. People take offense at those who come to tell them what they are doing is wrong, and laws are firmly in place to prosecute violators. With these rules firmly entrenched, how are believers to go into those nations and effectively promote Christianity? This is where the instruction, "Be as wise as a serpent, and as harmless as a dove" must be obeyed.

Wise, Harmless and Terribly Efficient

I have been inspired to see how one lady evangelist has penetrated Islamic strongholds in places like northern Sudan. With the government's approval, she has been able to preach the good news to thousands of Sudanese Muslims.

She begins her meetings by telling her audiences that Jesus loves Muslims, and that she loves them too. This is always a good way to start, because people like to hear that you love them. If you go to a people swinging a sword of judgment, they will throw up defenses and reject you.

The woman also honors Muslim customs by wearing a modest head covering. A blatant disregard for a society's customs will get you nowhere. The great missionary to China, Hudson Taylor, failed in evangelism until he grew a pigtail like the men he was trying to reach. Once he had the pigtail, people began listening to him. As long we don't compromise the Word of God when reaching out to a people, many things are acceptable.

When this woman preaches, she usually takes a text from one of the gospels where Jesus brings healing or deliverance to someone in need. After talking about the miracle, she tells the gathering that the One who healed people in the gospels is present to heal people today. She then offers to pray for the sick in Jesus' name. As the diseased and infirm respond to her compassionate ministry, the power of God breaks out all over the place. The Lord literally confirms His Word with signs following, and the people witness the work of the living Redeemer first hand. Joy and excitement quickly spread throughout the crowd as blind eyes open, deaf ears unstop, crippled bodies are made whole, and deadly illnesses are healed. It is then that many in the crowd want to receive Jesus the Healer as Savior and Lord. In her evangelistic outreach, nothing negative is ever said about Mohammed or Allah; in fact, they are pretty much ignored. Myriads of people, on the other hand, become eager to embrace the One who manifests Himself as Healer and Deliverer. Once the Holy Spirit enters their lives, bringing salvation, He begins to show them the absolute supremacy of Jesus, and they reject all others in order to follow Him.

Let me give you another example.

While he was ministering in Indonesia not long ago, civil authorities told a well-known Canadian evangelist that he could not preach the gospel for more than thirty minutes. They also told him there were to be no miracles.

"You would sooner keep the sun from rising," the evangelist responded, "than to keep God from manifesting His power when the gospel is preached."

Before his thirty minutes had passed, wheelchairs were being emptied, cancers were being healed, and a spiritual earthquake was shaking the vast crusade ground as Yahweh stood up to bless the people with His power. Everyone on hand, believers and skeptics alike, were overwhelmed by this display of Jesus' power.

God's miraculous hand serves to validate the Word His servants preach. Paul said that we are not to preach the gospel with the wisdom of words alone, but "in a demonstration of the Spirit and of power" (1 Corinthians 1:17; 2:4; 4:20). Miracles have a way of bypassing skeptical minds and striking deep in the heart of a people. When men's hearts are thus engaged, the Word more easily takes root in their minds. Perhaps this is why Jesus said, "Either believe me (what I am telling you), ... or else believe me for the very works' sake" (John 14:11, author's paraphrase). Often, those who have trouble wrapping their minds around the truth of God's Word are convinced when miracles occur. Although those who believe *without seeing* are more blessed than those who believe because they see, God will graciously allow people to witness His power so that they might more readily believe the testimony of His Word. I have seen skeptics change their minds about the truth when they saw bona fide and undeniable miracles occur.

Phyllis Outten entered our house one evening in the throes of a violent asthma attack caused by a condition called C.O.P.D., or Chronic Obstructive Pulmonary Disease. For several weeks she had been planning her funeral, and working with her husband to get her affairs in order. Her family doctor, as well as a heart and lung specialist at the University Hospital in Charlottesville, Virginia, had given her no hope, saying the time would come when her respiratory system would simply shut down, producing either a fatal heart attack, or a slow, suffocating death. Phyllis needed a miracle, and no man could provide it.

Phyllis' husband, Harold, was a skeptic. He believed in a historical Jesus, as well as in a future Jesus, but could not believe in a present day Lord who would heal sick bodies. He had adopted the cessationist view that the gifts of the Spirit and the miraculous power of God had ceased at the end of the early Church era.

On the night Phyllis entered our house, Darlene and I, along with our kids, had just returned home from a conference in North Carolina where God's power had been in demonstration. We had received an impartation for miracles, and our faith was soaring high.

I was upstairs unpacking when Phyllis entered our house. Within a minute or two Darlene saw her duress and reached out to touch her in prayer. Before she could say a word, the power of God hit Phyllis and knocked her to the floor. As Darlene and the kids stood around her, the invisible power of God began surging through her body like electricity. For twenty minutes Phyllis lay there, quivering and trembling under the hand of the Lord. He proceeded to drive every vestige of C.O.P.D. from her body. When He was finished, her strength returned and she was able to rise from the floor, although only with our help. But that is not all that happened. Every one of the amalgam fillings in her mouth had turned to a gold-like substance, and she was covered with what has been termed "glory dust," tiny metallic particles that resemble gold dust.

The praise service that erupted in our household that night was glorious. Phyllis was like the man at the gate called Beautiful. She merrily leaped and praised God for His wonderful goodness. In one fell swoop, He had taken her death sentence and torn it up!

When she returned home later that evening, Harold was skeptical. But when He saw that she was breathing freely, and that her fillings were all a golden color, he began to believe. But what really convinced him was the intense sunburn that covered Phyllis' backside from her neck to her heels. She had literally been radiated by the glory of God as she lay on our dining room floor! Harold the skeptic became Harold the strong believer. His transformation became evident by his bulldog tenacity to win the lost ever since that fateful evening.

Incidentally, the doctors who had been treating Phyllis' terminal condition were amazed. So was her family dentist when he examined her golden fillings. These professionals readily admitted that hers was a bona fide miracle, out of their hands and beyond their control.

9

The Righteous, The Wise,
And Their Works

For I considered all this in my heart, so that I could declare it all: that the righteous and the wise <u>and their</u> <u>works</u> are in the hand of God...
                                    Ecclesiastes 9:1, author's emphasis

The great work of restoration, currently underway in the Church, is in the hand of the Lord, and we must leave it there. We must be content to work with His agenda and on His timetable lest we become more a detriment than a blessing to His prophetic purposes. Barging ahead with only good intentions is not the wise thing to do in this hour of restoration. Godly wisdom, which gives direction and strategy, is the principle starting block. The city, regional and nationwide revivals and awakenings we desire will only happen if we "keep in step with the Holy Spirit" (Galatians 5:25, NIV). If we can keep from going ahead of Him or lagging behind Him, we will experience tremendous power and blessing from the hand of the Lord. In this hour, righteous men and women who tap regularly into God's wisdom and ply their energy to their appointed work, will experience His hand on a consistent basis. Pray that you be neither hindered nor a hindrance in this hour of restoration.

A concern many Old Testament prophets raised before the religious leaders of their day, was that they either "stumbled from the ancient paths" (Jeremiah 18:15-16), thereby inviting disaster to desolate the land, or they "stood at the crossroads" (Obadiah 14), cutting off the captives who desired to escape from the calamity their nation was suffering. The leaders (religious or secular) who hindered the work of restoration were eventually removed. Jesus put it this way: "You have taken away the key of knowledge. You did not enter in yourselves, and those who were entering in you hindered" (Luke 11:52). He said that the failure of the people to enter into what God was doing in their generation would be required at the hands of the leaders who stood in the way.

Archeological Discoveries

If the Lord tarries, the coming years will see awesome days of discovery and restoration. In the land of Israel, great discoveries are being made almost daily as archeologists uncover artifacts and sites of historical significance to the nation. These special finds parallel the spiritual discoveries presently being made by the Church's spiritual archeologists who are uncovering ancient truths and practices that have lain dormant beneath the dirt of replacement theology, religious tradition and the doctrines of men and devils. We should be thrilled by what they are uncovering and restoring to us. As long as their finds are not death-inducing traditions of men, or far-out discoveries that find no support in the Word of God, we should eagerly pray about how to utilize them for God's glory and end time purposes. The tendency of "the old guard" religious establishment is to fight what is recovered from the dust of the ancient past. Men used of God yesterday are notorious for fighting men used of God today! We must beware of this counterproductive tendency.

Jeremiah exhorted the Jews of his day: "Stand in the ways and see, and ask for the old paths, where the good way is, and walk in it; *then* you will find rest for your souls" (6:16, emphasis mine). The spiritual rest to which Jeremiah refers is the same rest the writer of Hebrews exhorts us to enter (4:11). This rest will only be realized as we embrace these days of unfolding revelation and restoration. As we come to Jesus, appropriating the rest He offers us, we also must be willing to enter into everything He is bringing out of the past. As we embrace these things, allowing Him to blend them with the ingredients of our future, they will become the very things to cause our success in every good work.

The Elijah Anointing: Essential for Restoration

Jesus referred often to the prophet Elijah. He, like others before Him, carefully linked Elijah's ministry to the last days, as well as to these days of restoration.

Then He answered and told them, "Indeed, Elijah is coming first and restores all things."
Mark 9:12

Around the world, Bible scholars agree that rather than referring to the literal man, Elijah, Jesus was here referring to the spiritual anointing that was upon Elijah's life and ministry. Although Jesus said that the Baptist was Elijah the prophet (Mathew 11:14; 17:12-13), Luke explained that John would minister "in the spirit and power of Elijah" (1:17), that his ministry would be very similar to Elijah's in its mission and effectiveness. Also, when the Word refers to the last days ministry of Elijah, as in Malachi 4:5, it is probably referring to the prophetic anointing that will arise on the last days Church. This is an anointing to turn the hearts of the fathers and children toward one another. The Church worldwide will become a fathering, mothering, nurturing community in the days ahead. The fatherless generation to be saved will need this special anointing to help mature it. As this happens, the spirit of Jezebel will get stirred up to a feverish pitch. I well remember how, in recent years, the feminists protested outside the stadiums where the Promise Keepers met. When men begin keeping spiritual, moral, and financial promises to their God, wives and children, families grow stronger and the feminist agenda grows weaker. The reason for this clash is as obvious as the nose on your face.

95

The Elijah anointing is also an anointing for signs, wonders and miracles. It equips us to prepare the way of the Lord when marvelous, earth-shattering events are about to occur. This world's masses must be awakened, and strong, undeniable miracles by God's strong hand will arrest their attention.

This strong anointing is also God's answer to witchcraft. With sorcery listed as one of the four major sins of the tribulation period (Revelation 9:21), the Elijah anointing will be imperative for pushing along God's end time agenda.

The spirits propping up the worldwide drug pandemic are the spirits of sorcery (pharmakia), and the Church as a whole has failed to grapple with them. These demons have ruined the lives of millions who could have become great men and women of God, and have kept them from entering the ranks of Christ's anointed spiritual army. The Elijah anointing in the last days will launch a major offensive against their strongholds and liberate millions from the sorcery and drug culture that seems so formidable.

As I sit in our family room, writing this section, several young adults are gathered in chairs and on the floor between me and the television set. As they sit here enjoying a Christian DVD, I can see how much they enjoy one another's company. Each of them is a brand plucked from a youth culture gripped by alcoholism, drug addiction, and rampant fornication. The strong hand of the Lord is also here this evening, preparing them for the last day's outpouring that will shake this planet with the power of God!

Another essential element being restored to the Church by the Elijah anointing is the power of confrontation. I will explain what I mean in the next chapter.

10
Elijah and the Spirit of Herod

Two evil couples appeared in Israel's history; both dominated by the female partner. Their names were Ahab and Jezebel, and Herod and Herodias. Both pairs were despicable, doing nothing to bring blessing to their nation, but rather a curse.

A young man named Elihu once asked the question: "Should one who hates justice govern? (Job 34:17). The obvious and resounding answer to that question is "No!" It is because the Lord desires to establish thrones in righteousness that He wants honest and good men in positions of authority. (See Proverbs 16:12; 25:5.) But because nations and their people often rebel against the Lord, bad leadership and the resulting desolation becomes the bitter cup from which they drink. Ahab's leadership was just such a cup.

Jezebel entered Israel with an agenda. By marrying Ahab, Israel's weak-willed king, she was able to grab sufficient influence to promote Baal worship throughout the land; and she was good at what she did. By the time Elijah confronted the 850 false prophets who served her agenda, all but seven thousand people in Israel had submitted to her idolatry. Even today, the Jezebel spirit is a master at getting the people of God to backslide and submit to all kinds of idolatry and sexual sin (Revelation 2:20-23).

The name Jezebel is stamped on human history as the expression of all that is designing, vindictive and cruel. The woman Jezebel was guided by no righteous principle, and restrained by no fear of God or man. Her passionate attachment to heathen worship and moral liberalism is legendary. She spared no pains to promote and maintain her sensual, idolatrous agenda throughout the land of Israel.

The prophet Elijah carried an anointing that aggravated

Jezebel and her husband to distraction. This mantle-clad firebrand boldly confronted Ahab on several occasions, castigating him for his compromise and calling him back to the God of his fathers. The prophet John, the forerunner of Jesus who carried the same strong anointing that was on Elijah, was also a burr beneath the saddle of his civil rulers. The evil couple of his day was, of course, Herod and Herodias. For his open criticism of their adultery, Herodias purely despised John, and yearned to see him eliminated. As Jezebel murdered the prophets of God in her day, so Herodias murdered the prophet of God in her day.

Many articles and books have been written about Ahab and Jezebel spirits, those malignant demons that have operated in the lives of so many people down through the centuries. However, none that I know about have been written about the Herod spirit. Perhaps it is time to unmask this satanic power.

The Herods lived and ruled in Israel for a longer period of time than Ahab and Jezebel. The spirits controlling them were just as mean and destructive as those that worked through Ahab and Jezebel many centuries before. Even though a widespread ignorance exists concerning this malevolent spirit, I believe I know where it is hiding. I also believe that in the coming days, the Elijah anointing abiding on the prophetic Church will root out and confront this spirit without fear. The warfare rising from this confrontation will be very intense and ugly, and thus, wrongly evaluated even by many professing Christians. Too many Christians believe that when Jesus ascended to Heaven, He left the Church with a mandate to be completely passive and non-confrontational when facing people who are being used by spirits of darkness. Rather than speaking up and taking action, the Church allows unbelievers to push them into the closet on many moral issues. A case in point: While the sodomites (homosexuals) are coming out of the closet, Christians are allowing themselves to be pushed into the closet. The Herod and Herodias spirits will do that to us if we don't take up the prophetic unction and stand against them in Jesus' name.

What is the Herod Spirit?

I believe the Herod spirit is nothing less than a major spiritual principality whose corrupting influence is passed down through countless demons seeking to influence, manipulate and control susceptible government officials in every nation on earth. This spirit was so successful at promoting idolatry and sensuality among political leaders back in biblical times, that Satan has increased his efforts through this type of demon for the age in which we live. This spirit influences many leaders to be men of moral and ethical compromise, with very little integrity while in public office. It makes mice of men, reducing them to the weaklings who allow aggressive and threatening special interest groups to dominate them in the political process of free nations! This spirit deceives people, causing them to "call evil good, and good evil; to put darkness for light, and light for darkness; to put bitter for sweet, and sweet for bitter." (See Isaiah 5:20.) Beneath its influence, men of political standing yawn and look the other way when sin and evil run rampant at any level of society. Let me give you some current examples.

In a large third world nation, where I was a guest speaker at a citywide pastor's prayer meeting, I challenged the men and women present to unite all possible forces for resisting Satan's plan for their city. When I was finished, a lady pastor went to the podium to inform the gathering about a sex circus troupe called "The Lesbian Bitches from Mars" that was coming to their city to do a "performance." The circus, she informed us, included abased and abused women (and the Lord knows who else) locked in cages, chained, whipped, and subjected to every masochistic, sexual act imaginable or unimaginable. The group's name suggests women doing things to women, but must also include men doing things to women, and to other men. Wherever the troupe goes, perverts by the hundreds pay to watch the atrocities, where occasionally, women who are nothing more than sex slaves carried from city to city, die in masochistic acts. The lady pastor wanted to rally the other leaders to do what they could to keep the show from occurring in their city. I detected a genuine Deborah anointing on the woman, one I learned was not appreciated by some of the men present. Similar to Elijah's confrontational anointing, Deborah's was an embarrassing unction, an irritation to those who wanted to look the other way when the Devil came into camp.

As I left the prayer meeting that afternoon, at least a few other pastors were talking with the woman, scheduling a special prayer meeting so they could find out from God what exactly they should do to combat the sex circus. But still I left the meeting asking, "How does a group like the Lesbians from Mars get permission to come into a city in the first place? Where are the city fathers when things like this occur? Where are the gatekeepers who are to determine what enters and exits their city?" I was told that horrendous activities like this occur through under-the-table payoffs to powerful government officials. When the Herod spirit controls such key figures, the sex show operators can purchase special favors. This kind of injustice occurs in every nation on earth to some degree or another.

Another prime example of the Herod spirit working through civil and government leaders in the United States was the 2004 rush by the liberal mayors in several American cites to grant same sex couples marriage licenses before the President or the U. S. Supreme Court could issue a decree to stop them. Any one of these godless mayors, themselves in bed with gay and lesbian special interest groups, could have been cast as Herod Antipas in the blockbuster movie, *The Passion of the Christ.* As I looked at the effeminate face of the Herod who mocked Jesus before His crucifixion, I saw the spineless and defiant faces of some of these mayors, "men" possessed with the spirit of Herod itself.

Who Were the Herods?

In the years just prior to Jesus' arrival to earth, and right through the earliest years of the Church, the land of Israel was cursed with the Herods, a dynasty of men who held political power that was corrupt and self-serving. A total of seven Herods lived and ruled by Roman appointment, and most of them were dreadful men who misused their authority and influence to gratify themselves rather than their constituents. As one studies these ancient officials, he sees certain characteristics that can be found wherever the spirit that used them is allowed to function today.

1. Herod the Great was the first of these men to rule in Palestine. History records that he was of a stern and cruel disposition, "brutish and a stranger to all humanity." Heartless and uncaring, he regularly executed those he deemed to be rivals, including some in his own immediate family. This is why he thought nothing of sending his killers to slay all the male babies in Bethlehem who were two years and under. When he learned from the wise men that another King of the Jews might be born there, he was enraged (Matthew 2:16). Many years earlier he had received the title "King of the Jews" from the Roman senate, and in cold-blooded jealousy he was determined to keep this title! But history records that he died not long after the Christ was born, no doubt judged and condemned by God for his cruel actions against innocent mothers and children. History records that in Jericho his death was accompanied by great agony of mind and body. I can only imagine the horror he experienced when a band of demons hauled his departing spirit into the bowels of Hades. I am sure his terror-stricken heart withered as he realized his fate. But it was too late for repentance! Hell has been his abode

101

ever since. Herod's realm of authority then fell to his three sons, the most notorious of these being Herod Antipas, who was given charge of Galilee and Peraea.

2. Herod Antipas was a worm of a man. As worms thrive in subterranean environments so Herod flourished within the activities of a debased human character. Jesus called him a fox in Luke 13:32, for he was a conniving and wicked man. Why did Christ label him a fox? The Song of Songs says that foxes destroy the vine (2:15). The Herod spirit will always weaken and damage the Church (Vine) when allowed to do so. Some of our greatest adversaries are the political leaders who pass legislation opposing Christ's mandate for the Church. Alas, the Herod spirit today lives and carries authority in many of America's courtrooms and policy-making chambers.

Jeremiah lamented the signs seen in a society that has such foxes "walking about on it" (Lamentations 5:18). The enemy is able to enter her gates (4:12); her priests and prophets become men and women of compromise and irrelevancy (4:13); the blood of innocents is shed in her midst (4:13-14); the people lose respect for civil and spiritual authorities (4:16); her inheritance is turned over to aliens, and her houses to foreigners (5:2); her women become like widows because husbands are not present to support and protect them (5:3); her children become like orphans because they are raised without fathers (5:3); drinking water is purchased at a ridiculous price, and so is the fuel which warms the people (5:4); there are no deliverers, no heroes among the people (5:8); her people move ever closer to the scourge of famine (5:10); her women and maidens are ravished, disrespected and disenfranchised (5:11; her princes are hung up by the thumbs (5:12); the aged are no longer honored (5:12); her young men become slaves to heartless masters, be they people or addictions (5:13); dignified leaders no longer decide issues directing the nation, and young men no longer rejoice in the freedom and excitement of youth (5:14); and finally, the heart of her people grows faint, their eyes grow dim, and personal, regional and national vision is lost (5:17). Such are the results of a fox in high places!

Foxes also steal the life of feeble lambs. The same baby-killing demon that possessed his father dwelt in Herod Antipas; only it didn't have a reason to show itself as when his father ruled. Given the right circumstances, however, Herod Antipas would surely have been as ruthless and desperate as his father! Alas, the same murderous demons that worked through these despicable men yet influence politicians and judges today who support the right of women to abort their unborn children.

Antipas was also an adulterer. He had sexual relations with his brother's wife, Herodias. John the Baptist decried this sin to his face, but like so many government elitists, Herod remained in his ungodly relationship. How many political leaders today have a mistress or two on the side? How many senators, congressmen, governors or judges, use their political power to gain special favors from the elite pool of political groupies that orbits Capitol Hill? We'd be shocked if we knew. Maybe we wouldn't. We will know soon enough, however, because the Elijah anointing will soon jerk the wraps off these scoundrels and they will be exposed. Those who repent and embrace the cross will be spared. Those who do not will experience shame, embarrassment and hardship like they never knew before. In coming days, God will require many politicians to ante up. The stakes for being unethical and immoral persons with political power will be high! As judgment on sin has been increasing against leadership in the Church in recent years, so it will abound against corrupt political personalities. If judgment begins first with the people of God, and will only increase as the end approaches, then "what will be the end of those who do not obey the gospel of

God?" (1 Peter 4:17).

Herod Antipas was also a murderer of prophets. Although he did not really desire to silence John through death, he allowed his wicked lover to take off the Baptist's head. Generations earlier, Ahab did the same thing. He stepped back and allowed his wife, Jezebel, to kill the prophets of God who opposed her agenda for the nation (see 1 Kings 18:4). Like these two henpecked fools from centuries ago, many of today's political Herods are in bed with the spirit of witchcraft. Feminist organizations, with aims to emasculate men, destroy family life, and change biblically based laws throughout western nations, are riddled with demons similar to those that possessed Jezebel and Herodias. Even though Herod personally liked John, and even had a desire to listen to him, his need for Herodias' approval overrode his good sense. The need to have the approval of feminists and homosexuals is always a hurdle politicians must overcome. Few of them seem to be able to get over this barrier to honest and righteous government. But that will soon change.[8]

3. Herod Agrippa I was another politician who persecuted the Church and withstood the purposes of God for the nation. He was responsible for the murder of the apostle James, and the imprisonment of the apostle Peter (see Acts 12:1-4). He thought nothing of executing his own men when they failed to carry out his orders to the letter (vs. 19). On the day he died, in A.D. 44, an angel of the Lord struck his bowels and filled him with maggots. His death was certainly painful, frightening and filled with agony; but the Word of God grew and multiplied (Acts 12:21-24). Ha! Agrippa's foolish self-exaltation had run its course and judgment had come! Today in Hades, that pompous despot begs God for mercy, but nobody listens! Oh, the foolishness of resisting the righteous Lord and His purposes for a nation! If they refuse to repent and turn their hearts to the Lord, horrible days will end the lives

of many political figures that rule today without the Word to shape their worldview and guide them. (See Isaiah 5:20; 10:1-4.)

Beware, Herod. The Prophets are Coming!

A time of great exposure is at hand. God's standard-bearers, the prophets, will carry the standard He is raising against corruption in government! These firebrands from Heaven will have more than mere words in their arsenals, they will have Holy Spirit power as well. Their words will inspire the remnant Church to get down on its knees in Heaven-piercing, earth-jarring intercession, and will provoke strategic confrontations with the forces of darkness. As a result of this governmental intercession, world leaders will begin to be converted by dreams or eaten by maggots!

Political leaders won't like the prophetic element in the end time Church; in fact they will hate it! (See 1 Kings 22:8.) But they won't be able to silence it either. Many school officials and antichristian educators won't be happy, because the biblical truths the prophetic Church heralds will find their way into the hearts of many young people, frustrating the liberal agenda socialist educators have been promoting for decades. Anointed children will begin speaking up and challenging the unscriptural bias the godless social engineers have been promoting. Perverted education associations will one day find that there are more fires starting on school campuses than they can successfully put out! Revival will smash hard into the decaying agenda of liberal politicians and educators, annoying them to distraction! How can one silence people (adults and children alike) who walk in the mantle of Elijah? How can one forever quench the effectiveness of living flames that gain more influence over their peers than robot educators?

Beloved, the battle for our children is intensifying, and will soon reach the boiling point. The heart of our kids is the high ground the prophetic Church must wrest from the human devils of liberalism and socialism! God's true prophets, equipped and impassioned for the hour, will not slink away and hide like burrowing snakes! Like Elijah, they will keep coming back, again and again and again! As God's hand of power validates their words and actions, masses of people will begin listening to what they have to say. This response will stir many leaders to a frenzied hatred! They don't like it when their sacred cows are assaulted and kicked over by Heaven's representatives. Persecution will then increase against the prophets, and in many regions, prophetic heroism will draw great animosity toward the Church. As a result, religious leaders will place tremendous pressure on the prophets and their congregations, urging them to soften their rhetoric and allow Christendom to regain the favor of the world rather than its sore displeasure. Many prophets and congregations will succumb to this pressure, but many will not. This will incite some established churches and ministries who compromise the truth to become the prophets' most virulent persecutors.

And what about the spirits of Jezebel and Herodias? What about the people deceived and controlled by these malicious demons? Those under their hand will be livid in the days to come! They will exalt their placards in the streets, and squeal like banshees in emotional speeches and press conferences that will be aired across the nations of the world. Not to worry though, because as the hand of the Lord comes upon the true Church in the final days of this age, their evil influence will pale in the light of His glory. The Lord will indeed empower His people to stand up to their hatred, and no power on earth will for long repulse them. Therefore, put on your armor, Church! Confrontation and warfare are upon us! Only be strong and very courageous. This spiritual war will be waged in the heavens, against principalities and powers, but played out on earth, in social, political, and military arenas.

As Jesus employs us, along with His angelic host, we will "plant the heavens, and lay the foundations of the earth" (Isaiah 51:16). With Jehovah Sabaoth leading the vanguard, we will invade enemy held territory, break the jaws of the wicked, and snatch the prey from his teeth! This war will be brutal and bloody. Many saints who enter battle will not come out alive, but neither will many who march for the enemy. God's strong hand of judgment, about which we will read in the final chapters of this book, will prevail as He quickens the Church for its end time mission. Because we are willing to preach this gospel and extend His kingdom "by life or by death" (Philippians 1:20), we will see the purposes of Jesus advance across the nations like a massive flood pushing everything before it to one final end. Indeed, God will soon consummate all things in Christ (Ephesians 1:10), and the spirits of Ahab, Herod, Jezebel and Herodias, along with many other malevolent, antichristian spirits, will be thrown down to perdition. While the princes of this world are coming to nothing (1 Corinthians 2:6), Messiah is coming for the nations!

11
His Mighty Hand of Power

The world is tumbling headlong toward the final fiery confrontation between the forces of darkness and the forces of light. Although it appears to be a reckless and frenzied plunge, we know that God has ultimate control and will not be caught off guard by anything that happens. In fact, His is the unseen hand that pulls everything to a predetermined end. Scripture says that He has "appointed a day on which He will judge the world" by Jesus Christ (Acts 17:31). This speaks of an *appointed* day, a specific time period known only to God Himself. The Bible also points to "the appointed weeks of harvest" (Jeremiah 5:24); to the brief window of opportunity when the Church will reap the mighty harvest planned for the end of days. And even as the armies of the nations rally against God's Israel in the latter times, His powerful hand will be that which manipulates the hook in their jaws, pulling them to doom and destruction. (See Ezekiel 38:4.)

Helping to precipitate these tumultuous days, Word-filled saints, with tremendous angelic assistance, will begin grappling with satanic powers that largely have remained unengaged in battle. A powerful thrust to win souls will be enacted by the remnant Church, and the enraged dragon of Revelation will fulfill that prophecy that says, "woe to the inhabitants of the earth and the sea! For the devil has come down to you, having great wrath, because he knows that he has a short time" (Revelation 12:12). In that day, "the blast of the terrible ones [will be] as a storm against the wall" (Isaiah 25:4), and the earth will reel to and fro like a drunkard (Isaiah 25:4; 24:20). Principalities and powers in heavenly places— the true location of the Devil's headquarters—will be agitated beyond comprehension, and God will slap a hook in their jaws and pull them to destruction. In reality, the groundwork is already being laid, and things will only intensify as the Lord's return draws nigh. Although Satan's army struts, threatens, terrorizes and lays every attack imaginable against creation as a reproach to God, Heaven's prophetic calendar continues to turn toward a cataclysmic finale in which Satan's forces will be eradicated and God's people will be vindicated.

Although Satan is presently showing his hand, his ugly hand, God is now revealing His arm, His powerful arm, for the whole world to see. A verse in Isaiah thrills my heart:

The Lord has made bare His holy arm in the eyes of all the nations; and all the ends of the earth shall see the salvation of our God.

Isaiah 52:10

When the Lord exposes His arm, the world staggers in wonder. When He extends His arm, His hand goes into action! When He flexes, demons are tossed to and fro, the powers in the heavens are shaken to the ground, and miracles are released to accomplish His will. *All* the ends of the earth shall indeed see His saving power in coming days!

When I read of the Lord *making bare* His holy arm, I envision a massive bodybuilder rolling up a sleeve to just below the shoulder and flexing up a huge bicep.

When I was a boy growing up in Norfolk, Virginia, my friends and I often went to see Granby High School's wrestling team compete with teams from other area schools. There was one wrestler in particular who caught our attention, and had our complete respect. His name was Joe Boone. By the time he was a senior, Joe was a three time state champion, and as far as any of us knew, he had never been defeated. Watching him manipulate an opponent was the highlight of our week during the winter wrestling season. But what I remember most about Joe Boone was his muscular build. He had huge, well-defined shoulders, a muscular chest, and

110

powerfully built arms. The sight of him sent cold chills through many of his opponents. We could see fear dancing in their eyes when they peered across the mat and saw what they were soon to tangle with.

Prior to his matches, Joe always wore a warm-up suit over his wrestling singlet. Even with the warm-up suit covering his arms and legs, we could see that he was a powerfully built athlete. As young boys we would eagerly anticipate Joe's match, because when he stripped down to his singlet just moments before taking to the mat, a collective gasp could almost be heard throughout the gymnasium. Then we would quickly look to see his opponent's face blanch with trepidation.

When Jesus flexes His muscles amidst the epic battles of the last days, His gasping enemies will fall back in every direction. He is indeed the strongest of all who possess spiritual power, for He is the one true God! As He shows Himself strong on behalf of this gospel, His messengers will not need the enticing words of man's wisdom to convince the masses of His Lordship. As the measure of the stature of the fullness of Christ (think of what I am saying), the Church—His body— will not depend on wealth or political standing to spread the gospel and reach the nations of the world. No longer will His ministers depend solely on past methods to advance the kingdom, because raw Holy Ghost power will be in evidence all over the globe. Undeniable, earth-shaking, and stunning miracles will settle the question of who is telling the truth, Jesus, or the countless imposters and prophet wannabes down through the centuries. God's awesome power will be declaring that Jesus Christ is Lord of all!

The Strong Hand of God

Whenever Jehovah determines to move
In awesome displays of His power,
He looks for a people committed to Him,
Equips them to face the hour.

His strong, mighty hand has within its sure grasp
All that His servants require,
To carry the day and press home the fight,
And saturate earth with His fire.

They take hold of God, submissive in prayer,
Embracing a grace that's secure.
They trust not their brilliance, their wealth nor their might,
But reach for His hand strong and sure.

The problems they face are stark and intrusive,
And cannot be moved by sheer cunning,
But molehills or mountains are nothing for God,
Whose strength is really quite stunning.

As Heaven's anointing pours down upon men,
Amidst boiling tempest and trial,
With love and true grit they impact the earth,
And drive back the evil so vile.

Though devils and despots prove vicious and stern,
And desperately cling to their power.
The time clock of God is winding on down,
To hasten their final hour.

Earth's teeming hordes now hang in the balance,
Choked beneath clouds of despair,
But millions are hearing God's loud final call,
The result of bold preaching and prayer.

He's sent forth His fishers equipped with His Word,
To cast nets with voice and with pen,
To find in their waters innumerable souls
Of women and children and men.

Within the full sway of Love so divine
Redemption for mankind appears.
It's free for the asking to all who repent,
And give God what's left of their years.

So now is the time to rally from slumber,
And shake off the dust of despair.
The Spirit is moving in waves of His glory
The demons are all running scared.

And in the bleak, grueling moments of war,
If glory seems distant or gone,
Stand fast bold combatant, have courage within,
For you Holy Spirit is strong.

So don't give up, brothers, and sisters take heart,
The King in His splendor now stands,
He'll soon mount the splendid white stallion of Heaven,
Crush Satan under His hand.

— M. H.

12
Awakening By War!

When God delivered Israel from Egypt, He did so by mighty manifestations of His power. The Sea parted, and the Israelites passed through on dry ground.

When He delivered mankind from bondage to sin and spiritual death, He did so by stunning displays of His power. The sky darkened, the ground shook, the temple's veil was rent in two, and the centurion at the foot of the cross, proclaimed, "Truly, this was the Son of God!"

When our heavenly Father concludes this age with earth-shaking revivals and awakenings, He will do so with irresistible displays of His power, healing, delivering, and impacting entire regions and even nations! And when He finally sends Jesus on the white stallion of Heaven, leading a celestial cavalry charge to gather His earthbound people to Himself, His omnipotent hand will perform astonishing displays of might and fury! Ours is indeed a God of majesty and wonder, a God of war; the lethality of the campaign that will consummate this feeble and twisted age will crush earth's godless armies, both visible and invisible, inaugurating a peace that will never more be jeopardized by the villainy of men or devils. But before that war to end all wars, the Church will wage a *spiritual* war that will reap a gargantuan harvest of souls into the kingdom of God!

In Deuteronomy the Lord asks: "Did God ever try to go and take for Himself a nation from the midst of another nation?" (4:34). Our answer is a resounding "Yes!" Jehovah literally rescued Israel (His nation) from bondage in Egypt (another nation), "by trials, by signs, by wonders, by war, by a mighty hand and an outstretched arm, and by great terrors." As it was in those days, so will it be in our day! Through a Spirit-empowered evangelistic army, God will wrest His holy nation, the Church, from the grip of worldly nations, "by trials, by signs, by wonders, by war, *by a mighty hand* and an outstretched arm, and by great terrors." Many millions of souls will be brought to salvation by the strong, recognizable hand of God!

While important and powerful men pit armies against one another; while false religions wrestle for recognition and influence in the governance of nations; and while scientists create an unfathomable supply of weapons for mass destruction; the Church of Jesus Christ steadily wages a winning spiritual war for the lives of men, one soul at a time. The weapons the Church uses are powerful through God, and are displayed in a wide array of manifestations. Daily, throughout the world, the Holy Spirit is convicting men's hearts as the gospel is preached. Also, great campaigns of mercy to those beaten down by life's battles are making an impact as the love of God touches the hearts of millions. But most exciting, the proliferation of signs, wonders and miracles, is impacting this planet more than we can possibly know. While men of peace lament the staggering proliferation of weapons of mass destructive (and this is good), they should be rejoicing in the proliferation of God's power to convict and save!

The great eighteenth century revivalist, George Whitefield, once declared: "The world is gripped in a deathlike slumber; nothing but a loud voice will awaken it!" In his thinking, the loud voice of which he spoke was two things: First, the tremendous volume he used to be heard by the thousands who gathered in open air venues to hear him; and second, the unavoidable convicting power of the Holy Spirit that seized the hearts of men and women as they heard him preach. When Whitefield opened his mouth to speak for God, the people responded like those who listened to the earliest apostles. Some were cut deeply to the heart toward repentance (Acts 2:37), while others were cut deeply in the heart toward an unreasonable demonic rage (Acts 7:54). Heaven-sent revivalists preach with an anointing that shakes up, wakes up, and calls for a radical response from those who hear them. As old Ravenhill often said, their messages either "create a riot or a revival wherever they go!"

Miracles: The Loud Voice

The loud voice God is using to awaken the masses today is the undeniable outpouring of Holy Ghost power through signs, wonders and miracles. In fact, signs and wonders *must follow* the preaching of the Word or we have no right to say we've heard the gospel fully preached. The apostle Paul stated that he had *fully* preached the gospel "by the power of signs and miracles, through the power of the Holy Spirit." (See Romans 15:18-19.) There is an element in signs and wonders that grips the hearts of even the most ardent skeptics. Through power evangelism—particularly in third world countries—multiplied hundreds of thousands are being saved as they witness a personal God with tangible energy who heals and delivers them while the gospel is proclaimed. In fact, as the following verse says, miraculous power is often the *proof* that God has chosen to do a mighty and lasting work among a people. If they will receive Him, and mix faith with the things they hear, power will be released to heal, deliver and establish them on rock solid foundations.

For we know, brothers loved by God, that He has chosen you, because our gospel came to you not simply with words, but also with power, with the Holy Spirit and with deep conviction.   1 Thessalonians 1:4-5

When Paul invaded Thessalonica with the gospel, he needed more than the power of reason to ignite an awakening. Because he went primarily into a synagogue to reach Jewish people, he needed something to show that his message was

117

valid. He knew that while the Greeks seek after wisdom, the Jews require a sign (1 Corinthians 1:22). Although Paul used his intellect to reveal what the Scriptures say about Christ, he also used raw Holy Spirit power to substantiate the Scriptures, "explaining and *demonstrating* that Christ had to suffer and rise again from the dead" (Acts 17:3). Whenever the subject of Christ's resurrection came up, resurrection power was always on hand to prove that Jesus was alive. If preachers of the gospel today would only believe God for demonstrations of His power when they explain the resurrection of Christ, they would see more signs and wonders than ever before. This would surely arrest the attention of many of the people they are trying to reach. In Thessalonica's synagogue, "some of [the Jews] were persuaded (by explanation *and* demonstration); and a great multitude of the devout Greeks, and not a few of the leading women, joined Paul and Silas" in the way of the Lord (Acts 17:4).

God's Hand *with* Elijah

Few people cited in the Old Testament experienced God's hand of power like Elijah the prophet. Although we studied some things about this man in a previous chapter, in this section I want to examine even more valuable aspects of his ministry as it relates to the hand of the Lord.

As we already examined, this mantle-clad eccentric, whose name means "whose God is Jehovah," boldly confronted the most powerful political dignitaries of his day, and none of his words fell to the ground unfulfilled. But that is not all that happened with Elijah. Astounding miracles flowed about him wherever he went. Like the Son of God who would later multiply the loaves and fishes, Elijah was instrumental in seeing a widow's food supernaturally multiplied by the hand of God. When sent to the starving widow and son in Zarephath, the prophet enjoyed a super-natural and unending supply of flour and oil that fed all three of them until a three and a half year famine was ended. At some time during his stay there, Elijah was also used to raise the widow's boy from the dead. It wasn't until she saw *this* miracle that she was inclined to confess: "*Now by this* I know that you are a man of God, and that the word of the Lord in your mouth is truth" (1 Kings 17:24). The boy's stunning resurrection convinced her, beyond question, that the man who had been abiding in the upper chamber of her house was legitimate and his word was true. Alas, people today are no different from that widow. To the world, the "persuasive words of human wisdom" mean very little. The masses are tired of the feeble homiletics of carnal clergymen. With a little preparation, anyone can spout chapter and verse. However, when honest people see the raw, unadulterated power of God in action, they begin to take seriously the message of salvation through Jesus Christ. Indeed, the most foolproof method of evangelism ever instituted is that of preaching the gospel with signs following (Mark 16:20).

Not long after Elijah raised the widow's son from death, the Lord instructed him to go to Mount Carmel and gather the nation to witness a toe-to-toe battle with 450 prophets of Baal and 400 prophets of Ashera. (See 1 Kings 18:19-40.) Baal was the male fertility god worshipped by Israel's ten tribes at the time of Ahab, and Ashera was a popularly sensual Canaanite goddess promoted by Ahab's Queen Jezebel.

The contest between Elijah and the false prophets was brazen; the atmosphere was tense as the showdown unfolded. Elijah and his opponents were to place sacrifices on their altars, and invoke the name of their respective gods to show their respect by fire. The one who answered by fire would be counted as the true and legitimate God. Needless to say, Baal and Ashera were silent that day. No matter how the false prophets leaped about, prophesied, or cut themselves with knives, neither god nor goddess could do what they wanted them to do. By the end of the day, all 850 were totally exhausted, as well as humiliated. I am convinced that it was because of Elijah's faithfulness to obey God and go where he was sent, that Heaven's angelic forces were released to bind up the spiritual princes of Baal and Ashera, and prevent them from consuming the false prophets' sacrifices.

When it was Elijah's turn, he painstakingly set his altar in order. After setting up his own altar of stones, he placed on it an ample supply of wood, and even dug a trench around it. Then placing his sacrifice on it, he drenched it with so much water that the runoff filled up the surrounding trench. Elijah wanted to make it as hard as he could for the God he believed would answer with fire from Heaven. He believed the Lord to be so awesome and powerful, that He could reveal Himself in such a way as to discard all doubts concerning His supremacy. By an act of war, God would awaken His people!

When the moment of truth arrived, Elijah confidently called on the name of his God. With bated breath the multitude watched as fire roared from Heaven and consumed his sacrifice, the altar, and the water filling the trench around the altar. It must have been a hair-raising display of Jehovah's power—thrilling on the one hand, and terrifying on the other. When the backslidden Hebrews saw the unleashing of God's mighty hand, they fell on their faces and unanimously cried: "The Lord, He is God! The Lord, He is God!" It is highly probable that Ahab also confessed Jehovah's supreme authority. As a result of this miracle, a national revival broke out among the people of Israel. Even though the revival was short-lived, by it God made a powerful statement to you and me today; and that statement is this: miraculous power always has the ability to awaken the sleepiest heart and turn it back to God! A well-timed miracle, which is an act of aggression against the will of Satan, has the power to arrest the attention of anyone who, for whatever reason, is not paying attention to God.

After trapping the false prophets in the humiliating contest, Elijah ordered that they be seized and hauled down to the Brook Kishon where they were systematically executed. This violent act presents a sobering picture of God's attitude toward idol worship. It is a stunning "sneak preview" into the coming terrible wrath God will unleash on all who believe and propagate "a different gospel," and worship at the altar of "a different Jesus" (2 Corinthians 11:4; Galatians 1:8-9). Only one gospel redeems, justifies and sanctifies fallen men. Only one gospel has an unending flow of signs, wonders and miracles to authenticate the truth. How can we ever dare present another brand to the masses?

God's Hand _on_ Elijah

Following the fiery showdown on Carmel's rugged heights, "the hand of the Lord came upon Elijah; and he girded up his loins and ran ahead of Ahab to the entrance of Jezreel" (1 Kings 18:46).

Prior to this moment, the hand of the Lord was not seen so much *on* Elijah as it was *with* him; being seen on the things he was involved with. The prophet had obeyed God's instruction to go to the widow in Zeraphath, and God's hand had come upon flour and oil, multiplying it. The prophet had challenged the prophets of Baal, and God's hand had tossed fire down on the sacrifice, consuming it. But now the hand of the Lord came *upon* the man, anointing him to do things that were far beyond his own human ability. How can a mere man outrun the best chariot horses in the land?

Two possible scenarios present themselves at this juncture in the story. The first one is this: When Elijah ran ahead of Ahab's chariot, he possibly did so as a special runner whose job was to jog ahead of the king, clearing his way and heralding his soon arrival. This practice was customary in those days. These runners were special men, capable of running great distances at a fast and steady pace, and to be a runner for the king was an honored position. If this was the case in this story, then Elijah was simply showing the respect due to Ahab's position, and not to his character. As a king and a man, Ahab was both a disgrace and a scoundrel! The task of honoring such an odious king would require that Elijah "gird up the loins of his emotions," as well as gird up his natural garments, for the long run to Jezreel. The task of honoring the king would require tremendous determination to bring every disgusted, bitter thought he had for Ahab into captivity to the obedience of God. This would require the hand of the Lord. Elijah probably felt nothing but disdain for this so-called king who had abandoned Israel's faith and yielded authority to his idolatrous wife. During the three and a half year drought that was now ending, he had probably wished a million times over that Ahab was dead. The girding up of his loins corresponded to the conscious act of mastering his passions and emotions, which were undoubtedly stressed. To show respect to a man like Ahab when you would rather shun him (or slaughter him), would require great assistance from God's hand.

The second possible scenario, and the one I personally entertain when I read this story, is that God's hand gave Elijah the *physical* ability to outrun the king's horses to Jezreel. Why he needed to be first to the city is not stated, but perhaps he wanted to be the one to bring an accurate account of what had just transpired at Mount Carmel. Maybe he felt the need to get there early, and place himself in a position to support the "penitent" king as he rode into town to face the hostile response and battering manipulation of a woman who was quite possibly the most vicious woman who has ever lived. Beneath Jezebel's withering gaze and hostile browbeating, the king might turn on his better convictions, and so Elijah's support might help him stand up for the God of Israel.

Whatever the scenario you choose to believe, a supernatural anointing was certainly involved in Elijah's dash to Jezreel. Why else would the hand of the Lord be mentioned in the text?

In the final days of this age, supernatural power will be released in the Church as it carries the gospel around the globe, and into situations that beg for a demonstration of God's hand. Gear up, beloved; in coming days the Lord wants to do amazing things through people just like you.

13
Girding Up the Loins: The Proper Response

Although God's hand came upon Elijah for an extraordinary task, the prophet still had to respond correctly in order for the blessing to manifest. In his case, the correct response was to gird up his loins for the run. Girding up the loins entailed pulling up the long, flowing garment that hung around his legs, and tying it around his waist so it would not swing loose around his knees and cause him to stumble.[9]

There are Christians the world over who fail to experience the full blessing of God's extended hand, simply because when He does stretch it toward them, they fail to respond correctly; they fail to gird up their loins by action. Let me give you two contemporary examples:

I heard of a man who for years bounced from church to church, asking good-hearted people to pray for and support him. "I need money!" he would say. "I need a place to live. I need miracles. Why won't God do anything for me?" At first, the people in these churches felt sorry for him, and bent over backwards to help him. They took him places, bought groceries for him, and even gave him money. But after awhile they began to notice that he did nothing to help himself. Even so, people continued to offer help, particularly those who had little knowledge of his history. One old lady even went so far as to rent an apartment for him, and pay the rent for the first several months. Still the man asked the question: "Why won't God do anything for me?"

A week or so after the generous old lady set him up in an apartment, a businessman in the community offered to give him a job that would only require a little work and a little time—about twenty-two hours a week. The pay wasn't that great, but it would have covered his rent and electric bill each month. With those bills covered, and food from the pantries of several local churches, he could have gotten by. But still he asked, "Why won't God do anything for me?"

As expected, he turned down the generous job offer. For no good reason he shunned the hand that was trying to provide for him. By failing to gird up his loins in this manner, he sorely grieved the Holy Spirit. After several months had passed and his next rent check was due, he had no money and had to be evicted. Because he failed to gird up his loins and respond correctly to what God wanted him to do, he was forced to return to life on the streets. Bitterness and misery continued to be his bitter cup, but it was not God's will, nor His fault. He had offered the help he needed, but the lazy man was looking for assistance that required no response on his part.

The second contemporary example I want to give concerning the need to gird up the loins is that of the many people who attend healing crusades in churches or public arenas. Many of them are very undisciplined in their eating habits, as well as in the amount of exercise they get, and if they fail to subdue the inner enemies that make them so undisciplined, they will not maintain freedom from the physical conditions their bad habits helped to create. The hand of the Lord will indeed fall on the sick in such Spirit-anointed gatherings, bringing bursts of freedom to their bodies, but unless they begin taking up the Word of God and developing a deeper faith, as well as the proper physical disciplines, they will probably get sick again not long after the meetings are over.

Let us again consider Samson (Judges 15:11-15). Two ropes already bound this Old Covenant warrior when the Philistines came swooping down on him at Lehi, shouting their threats. When the Spirit of the Lord came upon him, the ropes on his arms became like flax that is burned with fire, and his bonds broke loose from his hands. That was the initial burst of delivering power that Samson needed. But then *he* had to do something. The Bible says, "He found the fresh jawbone of a donkey, reached out his hand and took it, and killed a thousand men with it" (15:15). Samson's wise response to God's oncoming hand helped him turn the field of battle into Ramath Lehi, or, Jawbone Heights, the place where he could say: "With the jawbone of a donkey, heaps upon heaps, with the jawbone of a donkey I have slain a thousand men!" (15:16). Samson's wise response to God's oncoming hand turned a situation with all the potential for disaster into a field of tremendous victory! Indeed, when the dust was settled, God's warrior stood victoriously amidst the heaped up bodies of a thousand Philistine thugs. If Samson had not responded in this manner, by taking up the jawbone, the Philistines would have taken his life, even though his arms had been released from two ropes by a burst of Holy Ghost power. Beloved, God will do His part in bringing us freedom, but we must do our part in allowing the miracle to complete itself and be maintained. Do you understand this principle?

Elijah and Samson were not the only Biblical characters to experience the hand of the Lord doing wonders for them. Others also knew this blessing, *but only after* they responded correctly to the miracle God was bringing to them. Had Peter not stepped from the boat when Jesus beckoned, he would not have defied the laws of physics and walked on water. (See Matthew 14:29.) Had Peter refused Jesus' command to cast his nets on the right side of the boat, his nets would have remained empty, and a God-ordained catch would have been lost. (See John 21:6.) Had Gideon failed to gird up his loins and form an army, the Israelite's bondage to the Midianites would have remained for years to come. (See Judges 6:34-35.) Had the ten lepers not proceeded to the high priest when the Lord told them to do so, they would have remained lepers until their dying day. (See Luke 17:14.) Had the blind man refused to go to the pool of Siloam and wash the mud off his eyes when Jesus commanded, he would have remained in darkness for the rest of his life. (See John 9:7.) Had Samson not exerted himself "with all his might" after praying for strength, the pillars of Dagon's temple would have remained standing, and the lords of the Philistines would have lived to see many more days. (See Judges 16:28-30.) Had the woman with the issue of blood not pressed through the crowd when Healing passed through her town, she would have died soon afterward (Mark 5:25-34). Had blind Bartimaeus kept silent when Healing walked down his street, he would not have heard Jesus calling him to come (Mark 10:46-52). The text says "And throwing his garment aside, he rose and came to Jesus," and we know what happened next.

In all of these cases, the hand of the Lord produced supernatural outcomes *when* the people did something. But faith without works (corresponding actions) is dead, being alone (James 2:17). God will always ask you to respond *as* His hand is coming upon you. You may have to do something strange or aggressive; you may have to say something that other people do not understand; or you may just need to be still and know that He is God. Whatever you are called to do, the Lord will place a fresh jawbone within your reach. If your mission is to combat the demons that are attacking you, that jawbone will be a fresh, moist weapon with well-set teeth that won't fly out the first time you strike your enemies beside the head. The jawbone God provides may be a *rhema* word— a quickened word—or an anointed song, a prophetic promise, or a dream or vision that inspires hope and gives direction. Whatever God offers you, it will be white hot and lethal as you turn it on the enemies called doubt, fear and disease. Deliberately take up your weapon and use it in faith! Speak the Word over your enemies by faith and with hardnosed consistency. Hold fast to the profession of your faith without wavering, for He is faithful that promised! Your proper response to the oncoming hand of the Lord will ensure that the miracle flow has time to complete its mission and secure the blessing. But if you do not respond correctly, or if you respond in the wrong attitude—with little or no passion to see His will accomplished—then you will not see the miracle fully released or the blessing secured. The outcome rests largely on your shoulders.

Prayer

Father in Heaven, I thank You for the miracle flow being released as Your mighty hand comes upon me in response to my prayer. I receive the burst of Holy Ghost power breaking the bonds that would hold me tight. I have faith in Your ability and willingness to set me free.

In response to that burst of liberating power, I turn with bated breath to find a fresh jawbone with which to stand and fight. With this weapon I will fight, not to gain my deliverance, but to co-operate with deliverance as You bring it to me. Thank You for the prophetic promise that fills me with hope, the anointed song that boosts my faith, the fresh and vital Word that wins the day. With this fresh, moist jawbone, and its well-set teeth, I brace myself against the enemy and see the miracle fully unfold. And when the transaction is completed and the dust of battle clears away, I will stand in undeniable victory over the forces of evil that have sought my destruction. With faith in Your Word, and by my own determination to act on it, I turn this field of battle into my own Jawbone Heights, into my own place of victory. Thank You for Your strong and powerful hand coming upon my life. In Jesus' name, Amen!

Now brothers and sisters rise up and fight!

14
His Hand of Inspiration

The mountainous Moabite kingdom lay before the combined armies of Israel and Judah. Kings Ahab and Jehoshaphat faced a potentially disastrous dilemma. The hot, dry conditions found in the Wilderness of Edom, through which they traveled, coupled with the fact that they had been lost for a whole week, put their armies in a vulnerable position before the Amorites. The kings needed supernatural direction; they needed to know what to do next. So they called for Elisha. This fiery prophet had a knack for being in right places at right times. A strong anointing of the Spirit has the uncanny ability to place God's servants in such locations for Heaven's purposes. Indeed, when someone walks under a consistent unction, appointments with God-ordained destinies abound.

And so Elisha the prophet, up to date and as plucky as ever, was called on to address the situation from God's counsel. The Lord God will do nothing unless He first *reveals…*

> *But now bring me a musician!*
> 2 Kings 3:15a

Somewhere in his training, the prophet discovered the value of the anointed song. He knew that inspired music often sets the stage for the inflow and outflow of anointed utterances filled with godly knowledge and wisdom.

> *Then it happened, when the musician played, that the hand of the Lord came upon him. And he said…*
> 2 Kings 3:15b-16a

As Elisha came under the influence of anointed music, divine wisdom stirred in his heart. Out of the abundance of this wisdom, his mouth gave direction. "Wisdom is profitable to direct!" The kings' proper response to the prophet's direction resulted in a mighty miracle and the crushing defeat of the entire Moabite army.

This wasn't the first time that unction for supernatural utterance and direction came upon a man in the presence of anointed music. It has happened at various times throughout history, and occurs today as God's people step out to do mighty things for His glory.

Another Example

There was a time when a young king named Saul, newly appointed and anointed as ruler of Israel, came under the influence of the hand of God as anointed music was played. The prophet, Samuel, instructed him with these words:

After that you shall come to the hill of God where the Philistine garrison is. And it will happen, when you have come there to the city, that you will meet a group of prophets coming down from the high place with a stringed instrument, a tambourine, a flute, and a harp before them; and they will be prophesying. Then the Spirit of the Lord will come upon you, and you will prophesy with them and be turned into another man.

1 Samuel 10:5-6

The text reveals that it happened just as Samuel said. As Saul came upon the group of musical prophets, the anointing to prophesy came upon him as well. Through the hearing of anointed music, the Spirit—even the hand of the Lord—came upon Saul with supernatural utterance and words from Heaven. As this happened, he was indeed changed into another man. And until he became proud and defensive, Saul remained the champion of Israel.

The Prophetic Dimension Changes People

The prophetic dimension alters a man or woman, putting the heart of a lion within them. As we have seen, the Lord will do nothing unless He *reveals* His secrets to His servants the prophets (Amos 3:7-8). When we receive God's revelation, we hear the Lion roar! When we hear the Lion roar, then we ourselves are able to roar with authority! Frankly, every New Creation (2 Corinthians 5:17) should become a prophetic person of sorts, with knowledge and wisdom coming directly from the Lord. Through identification with Christ, by regeneration, and by the indwelling Spirit, he should intuitively begin to know about future things, and be gripped with a passion for the purposes of God. Worship, intercession, evangelism and spiritual warfare should spring out of prophetic revelation, and the gates of Hell should not prevail against him. When Saul encountered the prophetic unction, he went to new levels of worship and warfare. His campaign against Nahash the Ammonite, which was soon to follow, reveals this truth. At that time, the Spirit, or hand of the Lord, came upon him, and his anger was greatly aroused! (See 1 Samuel 11:1-6.)

Worship Warfare

We live in an hour when God is giving the Church anointed songs from Heaven. Both prophetic music and deep worshipful songs are being received as never before. We are not writing these songs so much as we are receiving them. Many of today's psalmists and prophets believe we are simply echoing songs that have already been sung by saints in Heaven. What did Jesus mean when He said, "Whatever you loose on earth shall be having been loosed in Heaven?" The Amplified Bible translates Matthew 18:18 as though what we release on earth occurs only after it has been released in Heaven. Could this be true where songs and prophetic words from Heaven are concerned? I believe so. I am not saying that every song is

133

from above, or that every prophetic message comes straight from the Lord, but I believe many do. Indeed, there seems to be a wide-opened pipeline running directly from the heart of God to the heart of the true worshipper. This is elevating us to new levels of authority for warfare. Our battles are being fought and won before the throne of God. If we really believe the Lord is in our midst when we gather together, then we must worship Him without fear, indifference, or stale traditional forms. Whether alone or with a host of believers, we must throw ourselves into praise and worship as if we have already crossed over into glory!

Psalm 22:3 tells us that Yahweh is "enthroned on the praises of Israel." Oh that the Church would comprehend what this means. When we congregate in Jesus' name, we have the opportunity to create what Dick Eastman calls a "throne zone," which has the power to impact entire communities, as well as whole regions and nations.[10] Miracles can be released in the shadow of that throne. From the center of that throne a wide and deep river cascades down in happy splendor, teeming with the blessings of God. And by the strength of that throne, an anointing is conferred that sends forth a holy army to do God's bidding on earth. Ascending in worship to the throne of God, the Church is prepared and equipped to descend in warfare and drive back Satan's occupation. One reason the Church for many generations has lacked the ability to crash Satan's party and alter society is because it has not known how to tap into Heavenly power. It hasn't known how to create on earth a throne zone through abandoned praise and on-your-face worship. The praise among many Christians has been far too cold and sophisticated. We have mistaken sophistication for reverence, stuffiness for godliness, and become far too restricted in our expressions of love and faith.

While it is true that some music should be quiet and reverential, some songs should yet be set to *Shigionoth,* or "wild, enthusiastic and triumphant music" (Habakkuk 3:1, TAB). Because our public assemblies are to be places where God's glory dwells (Psalm 26:8), saints of all shapes and sizes should at times feel free to "offer sacrifices of joy (shouting) in His tabernacle" (Psalm 27:6b). But too often we only create "solemn assemblies" (Isaiah 1:13, KJV), places where there is little joy, and no liberal expressions of enthusiasm.

Our high praises, the psalmist said, have the ability to grapple with principalities and powers in heavenly places, "to bind their kings with chains, and their nobles with fetters of iron" (149:6-8). Let the Church of today discover the raw, unfettered power of worship warfare.

Dead Services and Frazzled Pastors

In western nations, the typical Sunday morning church service involves two or three sleepy-eyed hymns, and a brief message from an exhausted pastor who has visited far too many people during the week. What follows is a mad dash to a local restaurant in time to grab the good booths or tables before the other churches in town let out and get them first.

As the primary worship leader in a church (worship is more than singing), the pastor, of all people, should come into the meeting refreshed from much time spent in the presence of God. Pastors should be brimming with inspiration that instructs and inspires their hearers. But fires are not kindled with dead embers, neither is enthusiasm stirred by burned out men. A little visitation during the week is commendable and beneficial, but quality time in the Word and prayer is most crucial. When pastors and teachers come to their pulpits parched and exhausted, no one is nourished or edified. Such pastors offer dry breasts to the flock.

Let us examine this basic spiritual principle:

Give them, O Lord—what will You give? Give them a miscarrying womb and dry breasts.

Hosea 9:14

Consider a woman's body. If nothing is happening in her womb, her breasts will not give milk. On the other hand, if life is growing within her womb, her mammary glands will produce the nourishment her infant will require once it is born.

Now apply this principle spiritually. If nothing vital is happening in the spiritual womb of a preacher, then nothing nourishing and life sustaining will come forth to the people. Across America this tragedy repeats itself every Sunday morning and Wednesday night. Hungry men and women drag themselves to church, trying to live on what their exhausted and empty pastors are giving them. The pastors are not the only ones to blame for this, but the flocks are as well. The American church has placed pastor visitation above the time they want him to spend in the Word of God and prayer. Congregations pay their pastors to visit them in their homes and in the hospitals, and if they don't do it as well as the pastor down the street, they are ridiculed and rejected. This pressure to perform is so intense that many burn out and leave the ministry.

The Bible tells us how a properly trained church should function. The ministry gifts of apostles, prophets, evangelists, pastors and teachers are to equip the saints for the work of the ministry. (See Ephesians 4:11-12.) The saints, in turn, who are inspired, spiritually anointed and equipped, should then infiltrate their communities, bringing the love and power of the gospel to the people they encounter.

When a complaint came to the apostles in Jerusalem that the widows were being neglected, they instructed faithful believers to appoint devout men to see to visitation and the food delivery that was needed. This was so that the apostles could give themselves "continually to prayer and to the ministry of the word" (Acts 6:4). When an anointed pulpit minister must continually run about his parish in order to keep everyone happy, he deprives the people of what they really need from him. If he is anointed to preach the Word, his

136

primary responsibility is to feed the sheep through his teaching and preaching gift, and not through visitation. Other leaders in the church, as well as gifted ministry teams, should see to that responsibility.

Most American congregations see empty altars each week because their pastors' hearts are empty. They may be compassionate and merciful men with wonderful personalities, but their hearts aren't full of a current word from God that will convict, edify or bring reform to the lives of those who hear them. They may put hundreds of miles on their cars each week as they faithfully visit their parishioners, but are they burning with a word that will liberate? If so, then their altars would be filled with hungry people, and their communities would be altered by genuine revival and awakening. Hear what the Lord says about this:

But if they had stood in My counsel, and caused My people to hear My words, then they would have turned them from their evil way and from the evil of their doings.
Jeremiah 23:22

The acid test, which reveals how much time a man or woman spends in the secret counsel of the Lord each week, is witnessed in the lives of those who hear them regularly. When the Word becomes a fire burning in his own heart, a preacher will greatly impact the lives of those who listen to him. Both inspiration, and the anointing to inspire, come no other way!

The Twenty-first Century: Days of Inspiration
Beloved, we live in the days of divine inspiration. We desperately need inspiration to speak, serve and to love, and the Lord is giving it! Although no one will ever again be inspired by the Holy Spirit to add a word to the Scriptures, God continues to inspire anointed believers to write and speak words that will move the hearts of men toward Jesus. Every

day, around the world, inspired preachers and teachers stand to educate and exhort the people who gather to hear them. Every day, Christian musicians and singers produce inspired songs by which Christ is honored and the saints are edified. Every day, anointed servants reach out to meet the needs of the afflicted and downtrodden. The flame of the Holy Spirit inspires their very actions, and people are drawn to the Lord because of it.

15
His Strong Hand of Revelation

In his book, *Journey Into Summer,* author and naturalist, Edwin Way Teale, described the speed with which a good naturalist observes the world around him:

For a naturalist, the most productive pace is a snail's pace. A large part of his walk is often spent standing still. A mile an hour may well be fast enough. For his goal is different from that of a pedestrian. It is not how far he goes that counts; it is not how fast he goes; it is how much he sees. [11]

As a Christian and Bible student, I like to think of myself as a *spiritual* naturalist. I find it thrilling to dig into God's Word and see what I can discover there. I like to turn over every rock, and stick my nose into every nook and cranny. And I really enjoy studying the otherworldly dimension of the Christian life. That is why the subject, *The Hand of the Lord,* fascinates me so much. I've been reading, pondering, and experimenting with this subject for months now. I want to know all there is about God's power so that I might declare it to this generation, and manifest it to everyone who is to come (Psalm 71:18).

My particular strong point—my forte, as it were—is the study and comprehension of the written Word. My wife calls me a Word Information Specialist. I don't enjoy reading the Bible through in a year, because that pace is much too fast for a guy like me. I don't believe I would see very much if I were to do that; I would pass over too many fascinating revelations. Instead, I like to walk slowly through the Word and enjoy the freedom of settling down on any given topic when it catches my interest. It is then that I gain my greatest insight into eternal truth, and the reality of spiritual things.

A man who surrounds himself with nature—the one we call a naturalist—loves to take ample time while observing his environment. Detailed studies of certain plants and animals in their natural surroundings fascinate him. With what he learns through detailed observation, he is able to relate in volumes to those who will read or hear him. Similarly, a *spiritual* naturalist is equally full and fluent. And if what he discovers relates to God's present-day power to impact individuals and nations, he becomes a *super* naturalist as well. He enjoys taking whatever time is necessary to fathom what God is saying in particular verses, passages, or books of the Bible, and in so doing, he better understands how spiritual power and truth might be applied to life's circumstances today. Therefore, for him, a snail's pace is the best pace, the most productive pace.

At a snail's pace I receive my greatest revelation into the nature and character of God. At a snail's pace, I am able to ingest, digest, and assimilate what the Lord wants me to glean from His Word. At a snail's pace, I better posture myself for supernatural communication with the Lord. At a snail's pace I better drown out the din of the world, and set my eyes and ears to receive supernatural help and insight from Heaven.

A Super Naturalist Named Ezekiel

The Lord strengthens us through revelation. More often than not, revelation comes to us when we are inwardly still and reflective, not when we are running about like a chicken with its head cut off. Upon the rock of revelation, God is able to build a strong and enduring people. Ezekiel was such a person. The Hebrew name, *Yehezke'l* means "Strengthened by God." Strengthened as he was, Ezekiel was able to endure hardness as a good soldier, and come to divine revelations and visions from the Lord. He was an Old Testament seer; a *super* naturalist whose snails pace approach to the things of God set him up for supernatural visitations.

Ezekiel was carried into Babylonian captivity during

one of Nebuchadnezzar's early military campaigns against Judah. Although action against his country, and particularly against Jerusalem, had shaken the nation, most of the Jews who remained in the land were far from penitent, and refused to recognize that the severe hand of God's judgment was in operation against them. Most of the religious and secular leaders continued to disregard the stern warnings that had been issued by eccentric prophets like Jeremiah, and so had done nothing to improve their standing with the Lord. Therefore Ezekiel was chosen to be Heaven's new messenger, declaring that a time of even greater judgment was about to unfold.

It is likely that when the Lord first came to Ezekiel through a series of visions, that he was applied to the hard task of digging and maintaining irrigation ditches near one of the rivers of Babylon. Whether he was resting or at work when the first vision came is not stated, but when the heavens opened up, the Lord immediately had Ezekiel's undivided attention. Read his own account of the event:

Now it came to pass in the thirtieth year, in the fourth month, on the fifth day of the month, as I was among the captives by the River Chebar, that the heavens were opened and I saw visions of God.

Ezekiel 1:1

Rivers represent the sources from which we derive life or death, blessing or cursing. The Babylonian River Chebar was a source of sorrow and vexation for the small number of exiled Israelites who were with Ezekiel, although it was sufficient to sustain the natives of Babylon. What sustains the world is woefully inadequate for the people of God. The River Chebar was probably that by which the Israelites, "hung their harps on the willows in the midst thereof" (Psalm 137), as they wept and remembered Zion. Into this bleak and hopeless situation, the Lord decidedly moved. What tremendous experiences Ezekiel had as the Lord came to him again and again. Read of his first encounter.

On the fifth day of the month, which was in the fifth year of King Jehoiachin's captivity, the word of the Lord came expressly to Ezekiel the priest, the son of Buzi, in the land of the Chaldeans, by the River Chebar; <u>and the hand of the Lord was upon him</u> there. Then I looked, and behold, a whirlwind was coming out of the north, a great cloud with raging fire engulfing itself...

Ezekiel 1:2-4a

How would you like to see such a thing? This priest/prophet saw visions of God that were almost too wonderful to describe! The entire first chapter is taken up with the prophet's vivid description of what he saw. In the midst of crushing despair for his nation, Ezekiel saw the glory of God descending out of the north—the direction of God's abode. "A whirlwind was coming," he recorded, "a great cloud with raging fire engulfing itself." This raging fire engulfed itself because, had the Lord allowed it, the flames would have broken out and consumed Ezekiel and everyone who was near him. Another prophet asked: "Who among us shall dwell with the devouring fire? Who among us shall dwell with everlasting burnings?" (Isaiah 33:14). The raging fire that surrounds God manifests His awesome glory. It is a fire of unapproachable light in which the Lord Most High is found to dwell.

By the Hand of the Lord

By what method did the Lord pour out visions on Ezekiel? The phrase, *and the hand of the Lord was upon him,* tells us. It makes a significant statement about the method God used to get His message to Ezekiel. The phrase, *and the hand of the Lord* also symbolized Ezekiel's mandate and authority for ministry. He was not going to act on his own initiative or by his own authority when addressing rebellious Israel, but as God's representative, he would be constrained by the indwelling Word to minister to the people.

In like manner, when the Lord's hand came upon Paul at Athens, "his spirit was provoked within him" when he saw the idolatry of the Greeks. (See Acts 17:16.) The original language says he was "pressed by the word." The Word of God inside someone compels him or her to open their mouth and present the truth to those who need to hear it. The truth can be like a fire burning in the bones of the one who has internalized it (Jeremiah 20:9).

Elihu was the youngest of Job's friends. After listening to three older men spout a lot of psychological nonsense, he stepped forward and initiated his response with these words:

For I am full of words; the spirit within me compels me. Indeed my belly is like wine that has no vent; it is ready to burst like new wine skins. I will speak, that I may find relief; I must open my lips and answer.
Job 32:18-20

The influence of God's word in someone's heart has the same effect as fermenting wine locked inside a wineskin. Without the ability to vent, the container holding it may well explode!

As we have already established, *the hand of the Lord* was the method by which God gave visions to Ezekiel. If today you are a seer of visions, a dreamer of dreams, or a spiritual naturalist who regularly mines thrilling insight from the written Word, it is because the hand of the Lord is upon you. Our God wants to communicate much more valuable information to His people by means of these supernatural methods, but all too often He finds they won't accept His methods, do not care to hear His information, or do not want to pass on what He says to those who need to hear it. This must change!

Strategic Positioning

And notice how the hand of the Lord was on Ezekiel *there*. The word "there" speaks of strategic positioning. One must be in the right place at the right time, doing the right thing, if revelation will come from God.

A life of fasting and prayer helps facilitate the flow and reception of divine revelation. Fasting has a way of putting one's flesh in a position to better hear what the Lord is saying. "Is this not the fast that I have chosen?" God says. "Then your light (revelation) shall break forth like the morning...then your light (revelation) shall dawn in the darkness" (Isaiah 58:6, 8, 10).

The Power of Identification

The text also says that Ezekiel was "among the captives." This means that he readily identified with the plight of his countrymen. If a believer cannot identify with the pain and suffering of those around him, he will not be able to help them very much. Shepherds must move among the sheep in order to bandage their wounds and lead them beside still waters. Shepherds must love the people to whom they are called if they will be effective.

Redemptive Time Frames

I also believe Ezekiel sensed that he and his people were in a redemptive time frame. That is why he was where he was. Someone might argue: "Ezekiel was there only because he was a slave, and had no choice!" While that is true in one sense, I believe his positioning was just as much one of attitude as it was of physical placement. In other words, Ezekiel *chose* to be with his people in mind and heart, not just in body. Certainly there were other Jews present that day with rotten attitudes, grumbling and complaining horrifically as they labored. But not Ezekiel. As a dedicated priest and lover of the law of God, he had "power to hold himself calm in the days of adversity" (Psalm 93:12-1, TAB). Such a mental and spiritual posturing enabled him to see and hear things others could not.

Someone can sit in an anointed meeting—in the very presence of God—and yet miss everything the Lord is saying or doing. How can this be? Because his heart is not right, nor is it truly present. Like the Pharisees who constantly condemned Jesus for healing on the Sabbath, modern day Pharisees are unable to rejoice in the miracle of God's presence and power among His people. Their hardened hearts refuse to embrace the special moment the Lord is creating. People like these always miss the hand of the Lord as it moves to bless and impact a meeting. They don't expect anything to happen, and so never appreciate it when it does.

Faithful to Proclaim

When reading Ezekiel 1:3, we notice that the word of the Lord through visions came *expressly* to the prophet. Perhaps he was one of the few God knew would receive and herald His unadulterated message to Israel's rebellious masses. When God knows we will be faithful to preach His Word to those around us, spiritual revelations will be abundant. How about you, beloved? Will you declare His Word, regardless of rejection and possible persecution?

When the apostle/prophet John received the "little book" from the angel on Patmos, it was sweet to his taste. But then it turned bitter in the pit of his belly. How could this be? Because once the initial thrill of revelation left him, John had to face the fact that some of the people to whom he was called would reject what God had him to say. (See Revelation 10:8-11.) The threat of persecution turns off many people who think they want to do and say something for God. But unless one is willing to take the heat of persecution or the cold winds of rejection, he will never be one to whom God speaks *expressly* through dreams, visions and genuine prophetic revelation.

145

Let us examine another passage from Ezekiel:

So the Spirit lifted me up and took me away, and I went in bitterness, in the heat of my spirit; <u>but the hand of the Lord was strong upon me</u>. Then I came to the captives at Tel Abib, who dwelt by the River Chebar; and I sat where they sat, and remained there astonished among them seven days. Now it came to pass at the end of seven days that the word of the Lord came to me, saying...

Ezekiel 3:14-16

Again, Ezekiel went to where the captives were, and *sat where they sat.* Identifying with a captive doesn't mean that you have to get sick with him, or be broke like him, or succumb to fear and worry like he does. But it does mean that you are willing to step into the mire and pull him out. Ivory tower believers rarely help anyone. They sit in their towers and ignore the cries of the needy. They are too busy enjoying the good life to soil their hands in the redemptive work of rescuing men from Satan.

For seven days Ezekiel sat astonished with the exiled captives. For seven days he had nothing to say. Had he attempted to spout something "spiritual" it would have been meaningless. He needed to hear from God!

There are times in every minister's life when his ignorance, or perhaps his astonishment, renders him speechless. These are the times when we should proffer no pat answers. If in humility we confess our utter inadequacy apart from God's grace, we can expect the hand of the Lord to come and give us what is needed. Scripture says that God gives grace to the humble, but resists the proud. When we find ourselves feeling astonished with the captives, we should hold our peace and wait for the word of the Lord. In due time He will manifest Himself.

Seven is the number for perfection and completion. After enduring astonishment for seven days, the Word of the Lord came, bringing direction and understanding to Ezekiel.

> Then *the hand of the Lord was upon me there*, and He said to me, "Arise, go out into the plain, and there I shall talk with you." So I arose, and went out into the plain, and behold, the glory of the Lord stood there...and I fell on my face.
>
> Ezekiel 3:22-23

Because Ezekiel had put himself in the right frame of mind, in the right place, the hand of the Lord came upon him. In this special time and place, the Holy Ghost instructed the prophet to "go out into the plain," saying, "there I shall talk with you." The plain was an open place, free from restrictions and distractions. It was a place where unhindered fellowship could happen between God and His man. There, out in the open place, the prophet saw the glory of God, and was overcome by the power of His presence. This was no courtesy fall—he was overwhelmed by the awesome presence of the mighty God! Positioned on his face, Ezekiel lay totally humbled and submitted to God for the purposes to which he was called. As a result of this encounter, even more revelation and empowerment was given to the prophet to preach the Word without fear.

Ongoing Revelation

> And it came to pass in the sixth year, in the sixth month, on the fifth day of the month, as I sat in my house with the elders of Judah sitting before me, that *the hand of the Lord fell upon me there.* Then I looked, and there...
>
> Ezekiel 8:1-2a

Here we read another verse that reveals the importance of strategic positioning. Had the prophet been somewhere else, he would have missed the vision God wanted to give. Ezekiel says "the hand of the Lord fell on me *there*."

As he sat with the rebellious elders of Judah, the Lord gave Ezekiel a vision of the abominations they were committing in the dark, in privacy (vs. 11-12), declaring a horrible coming judgment.

The number six is the number for man. The sixth year, the sixth month, and the fifth day of the month, depicts rebellious man's desperate need for redemption. The elders of Israel and Judah were behaving carnally and invoking a curse that would eventually purge the evil from among them. The end result would be the redemption and restoration of the nation. Ezekiel was allowed to see all of this in vision form *when* the hand of the Lord was upon him.

Revelation: Fuel of the Prophetic Church

Divine revelation is the fuel the prophetic Church will run on in coming days. The revelation we need for this hour is locked up in the written Word, just waiting to be discovered by hungry disciples.

A couple of believers were recently discussing the frequency with which the Lord speaks to them. After expressing regret that they cannot hear Him as often as they'd like, they turned to me and asked how often I hear from God.

"I hear from Him whenever I want to." I replied.

"How can you do that?" they asked, with bewildered expressions on their faces.

"I hear the Lord every time I open the Bible and begin to read." I answered. "If I approach His Word reverently and in faith, He always has things to say to me. I may not hear an audible voice, but I always get little insights that thrill my heart. It is like the Lord is sitting there, waiting for me to sit with Him so He can begin speaking to me out of the pages of

His book. It is marvelous. And because I am given to this type of communion with Him, He is prone to drop prophetic revelations into my spirit even when I am not engaged in studying or reading my Bible. The one dynamic," I explained, "feeds and strengthens the other."

Spontaneous communication in the form of words of knowledge, words of wisdom, and the discerning of spirits, is heightened by our regular times in the Word. This also helps us to stay in the right frame of mind. Like Ezekiel, staying in the right frame of mind enables us to be useful to God. Rather than become bitter during times of hardship and trial, we choose to be strong in our trust of God.

16
How to Release God's
Strong Hand in Your Life
(Part One)

Because of the volume of teaching reserved for this important section, I have fashioned four chapters. It is my prayer that this will help you. Please slow to a snail's pace, examining your life by what you read. Your effectiveness in coming days will depend on your learning how to walk rightly before God.

The Virtue of Simple Obedience

Notable men and women who experience God's hand on their lives have one thing in common: they are found *where* they belong, doing *what* they are supposed to be doing. This presupposes that each has heard the Lord, and is aware of his or her unique assignment in life. It presupposes that they are seeking to obey the Lord in every aspect as they seek to fulfill this assignment. Obeying the Lord is crucial for success. Obedience to God's call is the soil into which God plants the seeds of greatness.

Zerubbabel was applying his natural abilities, pursuing the dream of rebuilding the temple in Jerusalem, when God's strong hand came upon him.

Ezra was attempting to re-establish proper worship in Israel. And God's good hand came upon him.

Nehemiah was engrossed in the work of rebuilding Jerusalem's broken down wall, when God's hand came upon him.

Rather than gripe and complain when taken into captivity, Ezekiel kept a pure heart before God. As a result, God's strong hand for visions and revelations was his.

Elijah refused to bow his knee to the popular god, Baal, and was willing to challenge the idolatry of his day. And God's mighty hand came upon him.

Gideon displayed a little more courage than most while his people suffered beneath the heavy heel of the Midianites. While threshing wheat in a hidden winepress, the Angel of the Lord came to him and commissioned him as Israel's next deliverer. And God's strong hand came upon him.

Samson made God's enemies his enemies, defeating them at every turn. Even in the end, his repentant heart and rebounding faith were the ingredients upon which God's strong hand of power came to destroy the Philistine lords. In death he killed more Philistines than he did in life.

While it excites us to read about the mighty exploits performed by these great champions, it may also frustrate us to think that a similar power is available today, but that few people ever walk in it. But God does not tease, and what He says we can have, we can have, and what He says we can do, we can do— if we want it badly enough. Although we may never outrun a king's chariot, as did Elijah, or slay a lion, as did Benaiah, we ought to be besting and outmaneuvering Satan in life's many conflicts. Although we may never carry away the massive gates of city, as did Samson, we should be seizing the spiritual gates of our cities for the purposes of God. Although we may never be commissioned to rebuild a physical temple, as was Zerubbabel, we should be effectively building living stones (people) into a spiritual house for God. Indeed, the possibilities for what we can do for the kingdom are limitless if we will use our faith and minister from hearts of love. What can you and I do today in order to increase the occurrences of His strong hand on our lives?

How to Experience the Hand of the Lord

1. The first question one must settle before he can enjoy life and ministry beneath God's strong hand is this: Do I really

know Jesus, and does He know me? Does the Lord claim me as one of His own?

Jesus gives a startling revelation in Matthew's gospel about many people who will appear before His throne, pleading, "Lord, Lord, have we not prophesied in Your name, cast out demons in Your name, and done many wonders in Your name?" (7:22). These souls will blanch on that day, because they will hear the Lord answer, "I never knew you; depart from Me, you who practice lawlessness!" (7:23). The "lawlessness" He addresses speaks of those who have a form of godliness, but who deny the power thereof (2 Timothy 3:5). Such folks deny the power of their Christian profession by not allowing the dynamic of holiness to conform them to the image of Jesus. They like the gifts of the Holy Spirit, or the power of God, but don't take much to the fruit of the Spirit, which addresses the loving character of God in their lives. And so by resisting the character of God and only pursuing His gifts, their egos become warped and their motives for ministry become skewed.

The Lord doesn't know a person by his superior knowledge, his unique gifting, or by the strength of his personality. Instead, He looks for a Jesus-like nature in His servants. Is the disciple becoming more like the Lord in the way he deals with other people? Is he becoming more pleasant with each passing year? Do the fruits of the Holy Spirit grow on his branches? Is there an increasing display of longsuffering, forbearance, gentleness, kindness and meekness in his life? He looks at the level of love a man or woman has before He releases His power consistently. He doesn't look so much at the results he gains through his giftedness or anointing. Jesus looks for good fruit from a good tree, not good fruit from a bad one (Matthew 7:17-20). A wise gardener doesn't look for sweet pears on a crabapple tree, or tasty pecans on a pignut hickory tree. If we truly are branches connected to a good tree, then we will bear the good fruit of that tree. But if we produce bad fruit, we should seriously look to see what tree we are connected to. Examine closely the spiritual and emotional state of the people you are connected to in life. Are they basically happy and fulfilled when around you, or do they always seem to be on pins and needles in your presence? Do you exude the peace of God in your spiritual fellowship with others, or are you guilty of disrupting the peace of the Holy Spirit whenever you are together? Do you encourage faith in others, or do they exhibit the symptoms of fear and dread in your presence? Do your words inspire praiseworthy and wholesome talk, or does everybody slip into gossip and criticism when you are around? If conversations turn negative, judgmental and critical in your presence, it may be that you inspire it more than you realize. Therefore, examine yourself, beloved, to see if you are connected to the right tree.

I knew a minister years ago who was as effective a soul-winner as anyone I ever met. When it came to preaching on the street or in the pulpit, the man was as stirring as they come. When people lined his altars to receive Jesus, a simple touch of his hand would send many of them swooning to the floor under the power of God. And these were not charismatic or Pentecostal people who were accustomed to falling whenever a minister prayed for them; they were rank sinners right off the streets with no knowledge of being "slain in the Spirit." No doubt about it, the man was powerfully gifted. But right on the other hand, he was belligerent, demanding, and hell to live with. A close friend worked in his office for a time, and she said it was a hair-raising experience. Many times she could hear him ranting and raving over the phone, or hear him cursing someone who came to disagree with him in private council. The man's wife was also a wreck, and her countenance revealed the truth of how things really were at home. Subordinates trembled before him, and equals avoided him. Eventually his lack of character allowed the weighty success of his gifting to crush him, and his ministry crashed and burned. The gifting God gave him as he started out years earlier carried him well, but eventually it was not enough to support all it created for him. This is always the irony of ministry, and one that must be guarded against. Gifting can produce tremendous results, but without godly character and the sweet-natured demeanor of Jesus to support the weight of those results, pride, arrogance and a mean spirit will flourish, and the fruit will not remain (John 15:16). The last thing I heard about that man was that he had disappeared, and everything he had worked so hard to build seemed to be swallowed up by the very earth on which he trod.

Beloved, when Jesus tells us, "You shall know them by their fruits," He refers to the fruit of godly character. Do they pass the love test? In what condition are the people who are close to them? Are they torn down, bruised and bleeding? Fruit never lies! While miracles may deceive people, and cause them to rally around certain flamboyant personalities, they never fool the Lord. You can cast out a million demons, and not have love. You can speak to a thousand mountains, and see them all tumble into the sea, and still not be known, really known, by the Lord. Jesus is attracted to love, humility, and honesty. He chooses intimate fellowship with the one who seeks to bear the fruit of the Spirit as much as display the gifts of the Spirit. A believer needs both in order to be successful over the long haul. But remember, God is more interested in one's character than his ministry. He has more concern for one's humility and obedience than his super gifting. The Lord is looking for the inner fruit that depicts intimacy between Himself and His servant. If the intimacy is there, the ministry results may not always be colossal, but the communion will be sweet. And the result of this communion will be this: Those who come into contact with God's servant will be challenged to live closer to the Lord.

2. The second issue one must settle before he can enjoy life and ministry beneath God's hand concerns the social standing he has with those outside true faith. Will their disapproval affect him? Read what Jeremiah had to say about his:

> *I did not sit in the assembly of the mockers, nor did I rejoice; I sat alone <u>because of Your hand</u>, You have filled me with indignation.*
>
> Jeremiah 15:17

Life under the hand of God is not always a positive looking thing. Sometimes it is downright lonesome and frightening. People will flock to a man when God's hand manifests signs, wonders and miracles, but when it empowers the man to decry sin, many will shun him. At these times one must be able to endure hardship as a good soldier of Jesus Christ.

The "indignation" about which Jeremiah speaks is a feeling of disgust and insolence. It speaks of disgust at the evil things evil people do, as well as the feelings of contempt evil people feel toward people who walk closely to God.

Solomon wrote: "The unjust man is an abomination (is disgusting) to the righteous, and he who is upright in the way is an abomination (is disgusting) to the wicked" (Proverbs 29:27). This verse pretty well sums up the sentiments prevalent in the world today. It seems that many who reject Christ's Lordship have an innate loathing for Christians who are trying to order their lives by His Word. It also seems that Christians are feeling a similar sentiment towards those who deliberately reject the precepts and commandments of God. While it is true that Christians are to reach out to the world in love, it is also true that our feelings of disgust at what we see the world doing are warranted. Perhaps without that feeling, we would accept anything that comes along, and would become far too tolerant of sin. We mustn't however, allow the sentiments of disgust to rule us or dictate our response to the sin around us, for it will only be the love, forbearance and longsuffering of the Spirit within us, that will reach out and turn some of these people to the truth.

3. To have the hand of God today, one also must have a wonderful relationship with the Holy Spirit. A reason so many Christians never experience the strong hand of the Lord is because they are out of touch with the Person of the Holy Spirit. When we rely on our own brawn, brain, or our own money to accomplish the will of God, we always come up short. God never intended that we establish His kingdom without His anointing. Even Jesus needed the anointing of the Spirit to accomplish God's will during His three and a half year ministry on earth. (See Acts 10:38; Hebrews 1:9.)

The way I see it, there are three primary aspects of the Holy Spirit's ministry in us, which are necessary for the hand of the Lord to be on us in a consistent manner. All three are powerful and necessary. They are:

A. His indwelling presence. By this He makes us New Creations (2 Corinthians 5:17). He actually enters to make His abode within the person who receives Jesus by faith. This is the indwelling Spirit; this is salvation, and it occurs instantly.

B. The second aspect of the Holy Spirit's ministry in our lives is what John the Baptist and Jesus referred to as a "baptism with the Holy Spirit" (Matthew 3:11; Acts 1:5). This experience is subsequent to the initial indwelling, and is given for empowerment and the impartation of spiritual gifts. With these gifts (the Holy Spirit and His endowments), we are to become more able ministers and witnesses for Christ. This baptism doesn't make us better than anyone else, but it should make us better and more effective than *we* were before. This aspect, like the first one, happens instantly, and is entered upon by faith.

C. Finally, there is the aspect of "the fullness of the Spirit," or "being filled with the Spirit." This is not an instant occurrence, but a progressive blessing. It is the Spirit-filled life. It is ongoing and deep—much deeper than the baptism with the Holy Spirit, which can be experienced at, or at some time after conversion. The fullness of the Spirit is not the shallow rapids of youthful, untested Christianity, but is the deep and calm waters of a mature life wholly given to God. As a believer yields more and more to God, the Holy Spirit occupies more and more of his life, filling him until he is brimming over with the very fullness of God.

17

How to Release God's Strong Hand in Your Life (Part Two)

When the power, anointing and wisdom of God increase in one's life, enabling him to accomplish feats of service that are above and beyond his natural ability, it can rightly be said that he has been aided by the strong hand of the Lord. In the previous chapter we began examining the ways one can release God's hand into his life and ministry. In this chapter we will continue this important study.

4. To have the strong hand of God abide on your life, discover and stay in your unique gifting. Everybody has at least one gift. Ours is to discover what special aptitudes God has placed inside us. Is there a skill, developed or undeveloped, that brings you joy and a sense of fulfillment when you lean into it? When you consider service in God's kingdom, what causes your spirit to purr like a finely tuned engine? That may be a clue. But then ask yourself, "When I ply my energy to that task, do people receive from me? Do they take me seriously?" If not, it could be because you are not really gifted to do what you are trying to do, or you are behaving in a way that undermines your gift. When we force a ministry that God hasn't given us, or that people are not willing to receive, it is like trying to force-feed a trash compactor. Unless we have the key that opens and operates the compactor, we will not be able to place anything inside. God-given gifts, as well as the manner in which we offer our gifts, are the keys that unlock the hearts of people, opening them up to receive from us. And even if they rebel against the ministries we bring, as they did Jeremiah's ministry in his day, they will have to admit that prophets have

been among them.

I also think it is important for each of us to become comfortable in our own skin, and not somebody else's skin. Beloved, who has God created *you* to be? Never allow someone else to decree your gifting. They may help you discover and flow in it, but they cannot decide what it is. That is the Lord's job. Also, never allow someone to strap you down with a major job that does not match your special gifting. When king Saul attempted to place his own armor on David, the young shepherd rejected it and stayed with what worked for him. David's special gift enabled him to sling stones with deadeye accuracy. Saul's armor would have gotten him killed on the day he went out against Goliath!

5. To have the hand of the Lord, one must be prepared to both *hear* and *do* the Word of God. Ezra prepared his heart to seek God's Law, to apply to his life what he discovered, and to teach statutes and ordinances in Israel (Ezra 7:10). He enjoyed God's good hand of blessing as a result. As Jesus emphasized in Luke 6:46-49, the difference between hearing and doing, and hearing and not doing the Word of God, is as different as night and day. Our response to the Word we hear lays the path to either victory or defeat in life. James compared a faith that has no corresponding actions to a body that has no spirit (James 2:26)). Such a thing is nothing more than a corpse! Corpses are put in boxes and placed in forgotten, out-of-the-way places like graves or mausoleums. Beloved, let us be sure to be *doers* of the Word we hear, or we too will be left in forgotten, out-of-the-way places. If we refuse to *do* the Word we hear, we will never see the hand of the Lord rest strongly on our lives and ministries. Without applying the teaching we get from the Bible, we will be left to insignificant, isolated realms of existence.

6. To have the hand of God today, one must also display some courage—but not just any courage. It must be the right kind

of courage. What do I mean by this? The boldness some have to transgress righteousness and violate moral and civil law garners no favor from Jesus. I knew a man who had the nerve to sneak into people's homes at night and rob them blind, but when it came to living for righteousness and truth, he was a lily-livered coward! What his friends would think or say about him if he turned his life over to Christ weighed more heavily on his mind than what Jesus would say and think about him if he remained in his sin. I knew another man who had the nerve to jump from high bridges into churning waters, or climb the sheer faces of giant cliffs, risking a free fall to the rocks below, but when he considered becoming a Christian, he lacked the spiritual nerve to live for God in front of his daredevil buddies. That is no bravery at all! The Lord looks for those who will stand up for what is right, and do what *He* says to do, even when it cuts across the grain of popular opinion.

Courage to obey God in little things always creates the courage to obey him in big ones. Courage attracts the Holy Spirit, just as fear attracts the Devil. When the Holy Spirit responds to courage, He adds His own insight to the equation, enabling His servants to know things they could not know on their own. When the Holy Spirit responds to courage, He adds His own strength to the equation, making it possible for His servants to do what otherwise would be impossible.

Courage is not the absence of fear in crisis situations, but is that quality of spirit that enables us to face down our fears, scale the insurmountable, achieve the impossible, and defeat the indomitable—or die trying.

Several spiritual qualities produce courage in a person. They are one's fear of God, his love of truth, his instinct for honor, and his sense of loyalty. Without one or more of these unique qualities in one's life, a man or woman will never breathe the rarefied air of the courageous.

7. To have the hand of God today, one must also respond to

His guidance. Recalling the people we have studied in this book, none experienced the good or strong hand of the Lord until after they responded to His leading.

The primary method God uses to guide His children today is *the inward witness.* According to the apostle John, a believer is assured of his salvation when he has "the witness in himself" (1 John 5:10). The Holy Spirit within actually bears witness with the believer's spirit that he is a child of God (Romans 8:16). Without this inner testimony one cannot know for sure that he is saved.

If the Lord lets us know we are saved by the inward witness, doesn't it stand to reason that He will also guide us by this wonderful method? When considering a possible course of action, I always check the witness inside me before I act. Do I have a strong sense of God's approval or not? Does the written Word support or oppose my inclination? Do I have a warm sense of peace in my heart, or is there a sobering weight of hesitation that won't lift? Does an exciting inner "amen!" ring in my heart, or is there a nagging anxiety or uneasiness that hangs on me? I usually avoid action if one feeling doesn't eliminate the other. When I'm confused or uncertain, I wait. If a hesitation or unrest persists, I won't do what I am considering. But if a calming internal peace, a green light feeling, or an inner "go-ahead," intensifies as I consider the course of action, I realize the inward witness is giving me the okay, and I go for it.

The inward witness can also move us more suddenly than that. For example: I was sitting in a service one night when suddenly my heart made me aware that something was wrong. I might call what I felt "an inner intuition," because abruptly I knew inside myself that danger was present. Turning to the left, I looked over my shoulder, but saw nothing out of the ordinary—just a lot of people enjoying the sweet presence of the Lord as they worshipped. I then turned back around to the right, looked over my other shoulder, and "Bingo!" I saw him! A loud-mouthed, intimidating, service-wrecking false prophet, well known in our region, had come through the back doors of the sanctuary and was looking for an occasion to seize the meeting. An inner intuition, a strong perception— the witness within me—had been right on target! I quickly motioned to a couple of ushers, apprised them of the danger, and they made a beeline to the man. Once he realized he was discovered, he quickly departed.

The second way God guides me is through *the inward voice*. This is when God's Spirit—the Holy Spirit within me— speaks directly to me in clear, understandable words. This is not a "feeling," or an inner sense, like the inward witness, but rather a voice with certain authority. Sometimes it is very soft and gentle, as in a "still small voice" (2 Kings 19:12; Isaiah 30:21), but sometimes it is very loud and authoritative.

When I receive words of knowledge (1 Corinthians 12:8) they come either by the inward witness or by the inward voice. When by the inward witness I usually get impressions, and am suddenly aware of things I could not know were God not communicating to me. When words of knowledge come by the inward voice, I hear more specific details, and the names of people and their conditions come to me. When I call them out, people always respond.

God also uses a man's conscience to guide him. Conscience is the voice of our own human spirit. If one is born again, his conscience is a safe guide. When I do something wrong, my conscience immediately hurts me. My born again spirit—the hidden man of the heart—does not like it when I sin. When my flesh rises up to take control, and I say or do something stupid, my conscience reacts. If I don't stop it and repent, I become miserable until I do.

I took a little bottle jack from an old outbuilding one time when I was still farming for a living. Immediately I knew that I was in the wrong, *but I wanted that jack!* No one lived or worked the old farm at the time, and I knew nobody would miss it, but I still couldn't justify my action. As I drove home, my conscience beat me to pieces. It wasn't until I returned the jack to its proper place in the building that I got relief. Once I put it back where it belonged, joy and peace flooded my heart, and I was moved to a new level in God. As I look back, I can see that I passed a very important test that day, one that many would deem insignificant. But to me it was vital and life changing. Beloved, it's the little areas of obedience that the Lord notices in our lives. If He can trust us to do what is right in small matters, He will trust us in big ones.

8. To have the strong hand of God, one must also be burdened to see His will done. There is not one scriptural example of His power coming on a person who has an apathetic attitude toward God's purposes being fulfilled. Zerubbabel, Ezra and Nehemiah were so thoroughly committed to the accomplishment of God's will for Israel, that no amount of opposition could deter them. The Lord's hand always comes upon those whose passions run deep into His purposes. Jesus Himself set His face like flint to go to Jerusalem. His disciples, and even His own flesh, pressured Him to avoid the persecution that awaited Him there, but He would not turn aside.

Paul understood this principle as well. He said, "I press toward the goal for the prize of the upward call of God in Christ Jesus" (Philippians 3:14, NAS). As a result he was able to finish his race, as well as write nearly a third of the New Testament.

The pursuit of godly goals nearly always brings tension and opposition to our lives. If we find ourselves on a path that has no obstacles to overcome, the path probably leads to nowhere. The fact that we must "press toward" reveals that we cannot coast into the fulfillment of our dreams. We must press through every hindrance! We must get over every obstacle! Remember, no athlete is crowned but in the sweat of his brow; and no warrior achieves victory but in the din of battle! It is a hard rule of life that no goal is ever achieved without meeting and surmounting endless obstacles that arise to test the skill of a man's hand, the quality of his courage, and the endurance of his faith.

9. Take every opportunity to humble yourself.

This was the advice given me by a venerable old saint of God when I asked him for a nugget of wisdom that would hold me close to God for the rest of my life. For decades the man had demonstrated the very advice he was giving me as we stood on a hill, overlooking the little valley I live in. What a simple yet profound reality he shared, one I wish every young Christian could grasp. Humility attracts the Lord like few other qualities in mankind. Scripture says that the Lord "resists the proud, but gives grace to the humble" (1 Peter 5:5). Grace is the limitless and unrelenting blessing that crowns someone when humility characterizes his life. St. Augustine said, "There is something in humility which strangely exalts the heart."

Humility should be reflected in an abiding polite manner, and expressed in a consistent kind treatment of others. Humility makes a man accessible, encourages effective communication, and promotes loyalty. The truly humble person assumes no airs of intellectual superiority or authority; in fact, he recognizes that a vast sea of the unknown surrounds his tiny island of knowledge and understanding. To the humble person, anything like publicity, notoriety or display is quite painful. Let me give you two stirring examples of what I am talking about.

During the American Civil War, when General Robert E. Lee's soldiers were in winter quarters (1864), the General accompanied Confederate President, Jefferson Davis, on a tour of the camps near Richmond. One soldier recalls that particular day:

It was the afternoon of a winter's day and we were lounging in front of our tents, or rather huts, when President Davis and Gen. R. E. Lee came riding along the line. As soon as Lee was recognized the inevitable shout went up, a "Rebel yell." President Davis' hat was off, and he bowed right and left at the boys. But Lee sat like a stone man on his horse, never turning his head to the right or left. Apparently he heard not a sound. I was standing by our colonel, and turning to me, the latter said: "Notice Lee's humility; he knows the cheering is for him, but he passes it all over to President Davis." [12]

Following the War, Lee moved to Lexington, Va. to become President of Washington College. The following is an eyewitness account given by one of his students, which highlights the General's humility:

General Lee brought with him to Lexington the old iron-gray horse that he rode during the war. A few days after he had been there he rode up Main Street on his old warhorse, and as he passed up the street the citizens cheered him. After passing the ordeal he hurried back to his home near the college, and never again appeared on the streets on horseback. He took his usual afternoon horseback rides, but ever afterward he rode out back of the campus.... the demonstration was simply offensive to his innate modesty. [13]

Robert E. Lee's humility was a direct result of his strong Christian beliefs. Despite the revisionist effort to paint him in a bad light, he remains a shining example of what it is to be a humble Christian gentleman. He fought not for slavery (he knew and rejoiced that it was a dying institution), but for Virginia and her right to govern herself without strong Federalist intrusion, a fact that is ignored by many historians in our day and time. Lee's life remains a wonderful example of humility in the face of victory or defeat, praise or criticism.

But what happens when one leads a life of pride and haughtiness? What happens when someone gets too big for his trousers? A humbling occurs! In fact, it seems that life for most of us is a long lesson in humility. When God sets out to humble a man, He allows either Satan's kingdom or adverse natural circumstances to afflict him. (See 1 Corinthians 5:5; 1 Timothy 1:20; Psalm 107:23-30.) True brokenness should follow on the heels of humbling affliction. When things begin falling apart in the life of the proud, they should eventually turn to the Lord, seeking release from the devastation the affliction has brought. If they fail to do this, things generally go from bad to worse until they die. But this is not God's will. The Lord always desires repentance and restoration.

"Do I have any pleasure at all that the wicked should die?" says the Lord God, "and not that he should turn from his ways and live?"
Ezekiel 18:23

Do not be overly wicked, nor be foolish: Why should you die before your time? Ecclesiastes 7:17

The Place of Dragons
In prayer to God during a time of national humbling, the priestly sons of Korah lamented: "But You have severely broken us *in the place of dragons* (Psalm 44:19). What is this place of dragons? Is it a literal place, or is it a situation? I believe it is a situation—one where Satan is able to touch the lives of the rebellious.

John the Revelator identified Satan as, "the great dragon, the serpent of old" (12:9). Beneath the heel of this dragon one can easily be crushed. God will often allow this enemy to steal the health and welfare of proud and haughty

167

people. Eventually, the haughtiness of all men will be brought low (Isaiah 2:11-12). When this happens, whether it happens sooner or later, we should pity such people, for the place of dragons is a horrible place—even for our enemies! However, the result of this awful breaking can be glorious. Because when a man, humbled in the place of dragons, earnestly begins crying out to God for deliverance, he finds it! David tells us: "The Lord is near to those who have a broken heart, and saves such as have a contrite spirit" (Psalm 34:18). The word *shabar* (broken) means "crushed, split open, or quenched." It describes a heart mashed down, ripped apart, and out of touch with the comfort of God's love. Have you ever been in this place, beloved? Usually when someone reaches this point, little pride remains to repel the Lord. Often God allows us to reach this low point so that we will see both our sin, and our utter dependence on Him. Then He's ready to rescue us from the mess our pride helped to create.

The other word in this verse, *dakka* (contrite) means "powder and destruction." Have you ever felt like you were ground to powder by the pressures and circumstances of life? As a lightweight substance powder is easily blown away by small puffs of wind. When we feel this weak and vulnerable, we can no longer trust our own weight to hold us down; we can no longer look to our own strength and ingenuity to save us. Rather, we look to the One who has "gathered the wind in His fists," and can keep us from being swept away to oblivion.

The Camouflage of Humility

In natural warfare, the proud and boastful warrior rarely endures the field of battle. If he struts before his enemy, he makes himself an easy target. A sniper can pick him off with relative ease. I have seen this happen over in the realm of spiritual warfare as well. Many dynamic young preachers have allowed success to go to their heads. Many prayer groups have let success go to their heads as well. When victories begin mounting up in answer to our prayers, we must beware not to take the credit or touch God's glory. Nothing short-circuits the flow of God's power like an ego that is tickled with its own achievements. The most effective soldier is always one who keeps a low profile (in attitude and visibility), covering himself with the camouflage of humility.

Oral Roberts tells how, as a young healing evangelist with crowds swelling into the many thousands, his mother would often remind him to "stay little in your own eyes." This long-lived man of God was careful to heed her simple admonition, and God blessed him with more than half a century of successful ministry.

If you and I would have the strong hand of God on us in coming days, let us clothe ourselves with the camouflage of humility and meekness. Let us truly embrace the understanding that without Jesus, we would be absolute zeros.

18
How to Release God's
Strong Hand in Your Life
(Part Three)

I know but few Christians who don't want to be of value to the Lord. I know but few Christians who don't care to see His power displayed in their lives. The problem with many who *do* want to please the Lord, and who *do* want to see His power in their lives, is that they don't know how to cooperate with Him.

10. To have the strong hand of the Lord, one must be a God-seeker. Seeking the Lord is essential to productive Christianity! It is written that Uzziah, king of Judah, "sought God in the days of Zechariah...and as long as he sought the Lord, God made him to prosper" (2 Chronicles 26:5). This principle applies for us today. If we continually seek the Lord, He will give us good success.

As one seeks the Lord, his spiritual hunger-level increases. This is good, because if this hunger doesn't come along to encourage the seeking, then the seeking will stop.

When one first sets out to seek the Lord, he may not be hungry, but I have found that appetite for the things of God soon follows if he will continue seeking. Appetite may not always be on hand to get us started, but it will come along directly to draw us on in our seeking. Once we have it, we are hooked! True spiritual hunger is one of the few cravings that will not be satisfied with another solution; it must have God!

Seeking the Lord is also essential for a courageous life! The Psalmist declared: "I sought the Lord, and He heard me, and delivered me from all my fears" (34:5). A surefire way to drive out fear and create courage is to seek the Lord.

Seeking the Lord is also essential to a praise-filled life. "They shall praise the Lord that seek Him" (Psalm 22:26). The proof that one has been seeking God consistently is seen in the unfettered praise that flows from his heart and mouth. Show me a grumbler, point to a complainer, identify one whose praise is silent, and I'll show you a person who is no longer seeking the Lord as he should.

Seeking the Lord is essential for a vital and active heart, one ablaze with passion and fire! The Psalmist wrote, "…and your heart shall *live* that seek God" (69:32). I think nothing is worse than a cold, lifeless heart. Seeking the Lord remedies this sickly condition.

Being a God-seeker also garners the will and wisdom of God for any situation confronting us (Proverbs 28:5). We must seek His face in order to discern His will! If we never take the time to seek Him, we will frustrate our every effort at bringing His kingdom in our generation. But if we will faithfully seek Him, discerning and walking in His will for our lives, He will gladly release His wisdom and power at every turn in the road, and tremendous things will be done for His glory.

11. To have the strong hand of God on our lives, one must also focus on what Christ is doing in the world today, rather than on what the Devil is doing. The Psalmist learned how important it is to have the proper focus.

I am restless in my complaint, and moan noisily, because of the voice of the enemy, because of the oppression of the wicked…Fearfulness and trembling have come upon me, and horror has overwhelmed me.

Psalm 55:2b-3a, 5

Watching Satan's hand at work will overwhelm us if we allow it to. That is why I won't watch the news very much.

It discourages me. I have learned that my strength, comfort and direction *must* come from the Lord, and not from any other source.

Rick Joyner has called what Jesus is doing around the world, "the main event." On the other hand, he has termed what Satan is doing, "the side show." I like that comparison. When I pay good money to attend the circus, I pay primarily so that I might see the main attraction. Oh yes, there are other little things occurring on the grounds, but I am there to see the big thing! As far as I'm concerned, if I miss the big show, I've missed it all! Brother, don't miss the big show! Keep your eyes on the main event! Rather than spend hours each week watching worldly news broadcasts with worldly points of view, watch Christian programming that builds your confidence in God. Concentrate on the mighty things He is doing in the world today. You will better boost your faith by doing this than by dwelling on what the Devil is doing around the world. All that is happening in the world today—the terror, the famine, the sickness, and war—can be used by Satan to pull our eyes from God's purposes. We must be vigilant, for if the Devil can lock our gaze on his works, he will fill us with fear and hesitation, and not the faith necessary to triumph.

12. Another way to gain the strong hand of the Lord is by keeping company with anointed people who have strong walks with the Lord. Sometimes to do this we must press into their realm, even if they at first seem reluctant to have us around.

When Darlene and I were first married, we sought the company of an older couple who had been in the ministry of healing and deliverance for years. At first they were friendly, but distant. After awhile, however, they saw our eager hearts and brought us close. What we gleaned from them was a special wisdom and anointing to wage practical battle against the forces of darkness. What we needed from them would have been lost had we been timid and not pressed in.

When anointed men and women see that we are not after what's in their hand, but what's in their heart, they will be more inclined to include and train us. When they see we are more interested in what they have *learned*, than what they have *earned*, they will grow to cherish us as much as we do them. We must understand that successful leaders have already seen an ungodly share of parasites before we showed up, and some of these people caused them a great deal of harm. Why should they automatically assume we are different? Everybody claims to be honorable, but not everybody is. We should be willing to *prove* to leaders that we are different! It doesn't matter that we have great gifting; they want to see our hearts! They are not so much interested in our potential as they are our passion. Show them your passion for learning! Show them your passion for serving! Show them your passion for God! Young Elisha poured water on the hands of Elijah before qualifying himself to receive a strong mantle for miracles.

The writer of Hebrews encourages us to follow those who through faith and patience inherit the promises (6:12). The word *follow* could equally have been translated "imitate." To successfully imitate someone requires that you follow and study them closely enough to discover how they do things, and how they react to different situations. If we will be effective people at the close of this age, then we too must seek close company with ardent Christians who are fulfilling the purposes of God in our generation.

13. To have the strong hand of God on your life you must also plant the Word for it. What do I mean by this? We will only receive what we believe God for, and our faith to receive will increase or shrink by what we are regularly hearing or reading.

At age twenty-four, when I was facing the possibility of life in a wheelchair because of an aggressive form of rheumatoid arthritis, I deliberately chose to flood my eye and ear gates with biblical teaching on faith and healing. What I was doing was not popular among evangelicals back then, but I had to find the truth and establish my faith on something other than religious opinions. Had I listened to the people who said, "God doesn't want to heal people today," I would have succumbed to the wheelchair. But I didn't do that! Instead, I surrounded myself with teaching that filled my heart with hope and my mouth with the Word of God. Indeed, faith for healing (or any other blessing for that matter) comes by hearing, and hearing by the Word of God (Romans 10:17). I diligently studied the many accounts of God's power, as found in the Bible, and eagerly learned the dynamic spiritual principles that would increase the likelihood of my benefiting from that power. I also read the testimonies of those who have experienced miraculous power in more recent times. I allowed their stories to encourage my own faith for the healing I needed. When we fail to actively believe God for things, we don't get much of anything. Jesus said, "According to your faith be it unto you."

When a man or woman's faith is strong and robust, powerful words that unleash powerful results will be abundant. The Lord is not sitting in Heaven, wringing His hands, waiting for you and me to call out to Him to do everything for us. Rather, He is present, in the person of the Holy Spirit, waiting for us to engage His present power. He waits for men on earth to initiate things (transactions, activities, campaigns, endeavors) so that He can respond, involve Himself, and release power without illegally intruding or interfering. In truth, on our own we can do nothing to bring the Kingdom of God into a situation. But also, God has bound Himself to do very little on His own where His work on earth is concerned. He expects us to co-labor with Him by going forth to extend His kingdom prophesying His purposes, confessing His Word, applying our faith, and proclaiming His greatness. These activities will engage His power and anointing. The angels stand ready to hearken unto the voice of His Word (Psalm

175

103:20). Let us become the voice of God's Word on earth so that tremendous redemptive power can be released.

14. To experience the strong hand of the Lord on one's life, the sowing of financial seed is also vital. Miserliness is one of the final strongholds to be overcome before revival and awakening can break out across the nations. If God gives us the spiritual anointing we ask for, but we are still bound in the area of giving, we'll be unable to invade and conquer ground for the kingdom. However, when the heart of the Bride (concerning giving) matches the heart of the Bridegroom, awesome power will be released! We must be willing to *give* our way into an overflowing, end times outpouring. We cannot buy such an outpouring, but by supporting it financially, we show God where our hearts really are. An ebullient, generous heart is an open door we must pass through if we will step into the miraculous exploits reserved for the glorious Church. Giving with cheer, hilarity, generosity and thankfulness will create God's provision of power and finances for the days we are facing. If God can pass money through us, He will get it to us! God is eager to give His checkbook to a benevolent Bride, not a stingy old crone.

15. A universal spiritual law says that one is transformed into the image of what he beholds. In 2 Corinthians 3:18, Paul states that if we will behold the glory of the Lord, we will be transformed into the same image of that glory. What is referred to here means more than an occasional or casual glance. Instead, it refers to a piercing gaze, an abiding in His immediate presence. It refers to the consumption of His life-giving Word as one's daily bread. The written Word literally has power to change us from the inside out!

My daughter recently placed two large caterpillars in a dry aquarium. After several days of climbing on tree bark and chomping on leaves, both worms began spinning

176

themselves into large gray cocoons. What went in was not what would come out!

For several weeks nothing seemed to be happening, but we weren't fooled. We knew a transformation of tremendous proportions was occurring secretly inside the tightly woven cocoons. Hidden away and out of sight, grubby-looking, earth-bound creatures were becoming gorgeous heaven-made butterflies which, when released, would be able to soar on the wings of the wind. Rather than crawl on bark and feed on leaves, they would soon fly from flower to flower, feasting on succulent nectar.

Sure enough, as expected, the transformation was soon completed, and we watched with wonder as two beautiful butterflies emerged from their cocoons to greet the new morning. When we released them after breakfast, we watched with joy as they both flitted off toward the rising sun.

When we gaze at the things of God—particularly His Word—an undeniable transformation occurs inside us. We are changed into the very image of Jesus Christ! It is not something we make happen; it just happens! God's thoughts become our thoughts, His ways become our ways, and His power becomes our power. As we gaze into the perfect law of liberty *and continue in it*...we are blessed in what we do" (see James 1:25). This spiritual transformation makes us into the kinds of creatures who do exploits in Jesus' name.

So what do you spend your time looking at, beloved? Do you spend hours reading Better Homes and Gardens, People Magazine, or watching network television? Does an unwholesome hobby devour your time? How about a wholesome hobby? Even good things can become the enemies of the best things.

Do your friends capture all of your free time, leaving nothing left over for God?

"Come, let's check out all the yard sales!"

"Hey, let's go play a couple of rounds of golf!"

177

"Come on, let's go watch a movie!"

These activities are not bad things in and of themselves, but if they become time stealers, they prove to be Satan's allies. Your life will amount to little or nothing for the kingdom of God if you neglect sufficient time with the Lord in prayer and in the Word. But if you regularly take the time to plumb the depths of each Bible story you read, or do word studies, run cross references, make outlines, memorize verses—and be like the naturalist whose snail's pace gait allows him to really *see* what is happening around him—then you will soar on the spiritual wings of eagles. Remember, it is not always how far or how fast one goes that matters, but how much he sees! The more of Jesus you see, the more like Him you will become.

16. Another way to garner the strong hand of God is to develop your praise life. Ruth Heflin often told her audiences, "Praise until the spirit of worship comes; worship until the glory comes; and then stand in the glory." It is in the glory—in the manifest presence of God—that miracles are released.

When Peter's shadow fell on sick people in the streets of Jerusalem, they were miraculously healed (Acts 5:15). I don't believe that Peter's shadow actually carried healing power, but I do believe that in close proximity to this dedicated man, within a shadow's distance, healing power was known to touch those in need. A holy aura surrounds the man or woman who is totally given to God, and their particular gifting impacts those who come near in faith. The power of our gift should radiate from the glory within us, and touch the people around us. Spiritual aura has within it the power of the age to come! Heaven's power to heal and deliver throbs within the glory, and the glory is unmasked as we lead lives of fervent praise and worship.

I have one friend whose prophetic gifting spills over on almost anyone who gets near him. I have seen him open conversations with total strangers as they pass each other in public places, and within a few seconds, his gift has disarmed them and made them receptive to the word of the Lord that addresses the secret pain in their lives.

I have another friend whose powerful deliverance anointing agitates certain demons within those who get near him. Often, without his saying a single word, nervousness will occur within them, and the trained eye will see the demons begin to squirm. If he feels the time is right, my friend will then deal with the demons and lead their victim's in the way of truth. This man expels as many demons *outside* church buildings as he does inside them.

Do you understand what I am saying here? Your gifts, if anointed, should impact those around you, and a proper praise life will increase the effectiveness of that anointing.

Since the Lord is enthroned on the praises of His people (Psalm 23:3), every committed worshipper should create a "throne zone" wherever he goes! In the atmosphere surrounding the enthroned God (remember, His Spirit dwells within us), miraculous power should pulsate, touching everyone who comes with an honest heart to receive. Because Peter was an exuberant worshipper of God (he spoke of joy unspeakable and being full of glory), healing, delivering power emanated from him, impacting thousands. Jesus had said, "Out of your belly shall flow rivers of living water" (John 7:38).

One day as I was considering the healing of the lady who came to Jesus with the issue of blood (Mark 5:24-34), the Lord educated me concerning our responsibility to stay full and ready. "Your responsibility," He said, "is not to make everyone drink from the river inside you. But *it is* your responsibility to keep that river flowing fresh and strong, so that as thirsty ones come, they will find a flow that will meet their needs."

That word released me from feeling responsible for everybody. There are folks who will never receive from me, because they do not want to receive from me. I am not responsible for these folks. Even Jesus could not heal everyone who crossed His path. But I am responsible to stay in such close contact with the Father, that His power fills me and is readily available to all who seek it from me with the right attitudes of faith and humility.

At the time the woman with the issue of blood was healed, a throng of people pressed around Jesus, but she was the only one who received. Her faith drew healing power from Him. Jesus responded to her touch by saying, "Virtue has gone out of Me!" He actually felt a release of the river; He felt the tangible current flow forth. As He turned in the crowd to see who touched Him, He inwardly rejoiced that someone had come to drink. The healing was not so much His decision as it was hers. She pressed through every obstacle and tapped into His power. She risked everything to get what she needed. All Jesus did was see that people like her were not disappointed when they came. We must have the same mind as Him.

The habit of pulling apart to deserted places to commune with the Father kept the river flowing strong and pure in Jesus' life. It can be no different for you and me. The measure of time and devotion we give to the Father in praise, prayer and study, will determine the measure of virtue and power that will flow from us to others.

19

How to Release God's
Strong Hand in Your Life
(Part Four)

17. Obedience to God is essential if we will consistently experience His strong and wonderful hand on our lives. The prophet Samuel rightly said, "Behold, to obey is better than sacrifice, and to heed (is better) than the fat of rams" (1 Samuel 15:22b). Many believers do not enjoy the hand of the Lord in their lives simply because they have rejected some very important instructions He gave them in the past. They may jump up and down, praising well in public meetings. They may quote thousands of Bible verses word for word. They may even voice prayers that sound eloquent and powerful when they are among the saints. But if they have failed to obey instructions God has clearly lain before them, their spiritual activity will not be very successful.

Jesus asks, "But why do you call Me 'Lord, Lord,' and not do the things which I say?" (Luke 6:46). Sometimes in an effort to do great things for the Lord, we stumble over the essential "small" things, and find out too late that we failed because we have been disobedient. What you are called to do today may not be grandiose, but if the Lord has given it to you as an assignment, do it with all your heart and expect His strong hand to crown it with success. The Lord wants obedience more than anything else. If there is an obvious absence of God's hand on your life, it may be that you've been disobedient in some important area He has been trying to address. When we promptly and cheerfully obey, however, God's power is released in our lives, making us effective in

181

all that we set our hands to do. (See Deuteronomy 28:1-14; Isaiah 1:19; 2 Timothy 3:16-17.)

18. Staying close and connected to the right people is also essential to having God's hand on your life. Embracing headship and joining with other Christians who are fitting, functioning, and flourishing members of the Body of Christ, is a healthy thing. Going it alone is foolish arrogance.

When tapping the power of the Lord to heal his servant boy, the Roman centurion cited his own submission to authority as being a reason why his authority worked. If he couldn't obey and serve his superiors, how could he expect his subordinates to obey and serve him? He recognized that the same principle was working in Jesus. He knew the Lord was a man under the authority of Heaven's God, and that His authority would flow with only a Word. (See Matthew 8:8-9.)

In our day, God will only be pleased to reveal His strong hand through those who are part of a working team. Whether you are submitted to an apostle, a pastor, or to a teacher standing at the head of a major ministry, or perhaps simply to a team of peers with whom you can be mutually accountable, stay connected! Isaiah 65:8 says, "the new wine is found in the cluster," and that "a blessing is in it." A single grape, pulled from the cluster and lying on the floor, hasn't a thimble-full of juice within it; but a cluster of grapes, bound together and closely connected, is brimming with new wine! Little power and blessing will be found in the Christian who chooses to stay unconnected and unaccountable to legitimate spiritual authority. Little anointing will accompany those who try to do things for God apart from the help of others. In fact, such arrogance will soon be sifted.

19. One more way to garner the strong hand of the Lord on your life is to reject the notion that you deserve (or need) recognition for anything you do for God. Jesus said that if

you do things out of a need to be seen and admired by men, you have all the reward you'll ever get. Perish the thought that you might receive a pat on the back for a job well done! If instead you do things from your love for God, and a desire to bless and please Him, your reward will be great in Heaven. God may reward you here, but that won't matter to you.

The work of an unknown good man is like a hidden vein of water flowing quietly underground, secretly making the grass above both green and lush. People who lounge and play on that ground rarely ask: "Why is this grass so beautiful? Who is the good man who provided this for us?"

One of my favorite short stories in the Old Testament is found in the Book of Ecclesiastes. It speaks of such a good man who wasn't afraid of anonymity:

There was a little city with few men in it; and a great king came against and besieged it, and built great snares around it. Now there was found in it a poor wise man, and he by his wisdom delivered the city. Yet no one remembered that same poor man.

9:14-15

Our generation of Christians (at least those of us who comprise the remnant) desire revival and awakening probably as much as any generation that has ever lived. How desperately we want to see our cities and counties delivered from the bondages imposed by principalities and powers in heavenly places! But as the story goes, only wisdom—God's manifest wisdom—is sufficient to bring deliverance to our land. I think it is significant that the hero in this story was a man with only two things said about him, but those two qualities were sufficient to save the day for his people. First, he was a poor man. And second, he was a wise man. The fact that he was a poor man doesn't necessarily imply that he lived in poverty, but it does mean that he was poor in spirit. Jesus said, "Blessed

183

are the poor in spirit, for theirs is the kingdom of heaven" (Matthew 5:3). The greater blessings of the kingdom are reserved for such men and women. The poor in spirit relinquish the right to pursue worldly wealth, power or fame. As bond slaves to the King of Glory they pursue Heaven's treasures; namely, wisdom, power, and a blessed walk of fruitfulness. They know that in and of themselves they are nothing and have nothing to offer. But they also know that humility under God's mighty hand will in due course, exalt them over every frowning evil. They also know that *if* they utilize what God places in their hands, they will succeed in all He calls them to do. In the poor man's case, God's wisdom was all he needed to overcome the challenge presented by the evil king. "Wisdom is better than strength…Wisdom is better than weapons of war!" (Ecclesiastes 9:16, 18).

The strategy for victory that God gave this poor man is not stated, but we can be sure it was exactly what was needed. The Lord can trust the poor in spirit with the kind of wisdom that will pull down principalities over cities, counties and nations. Such spiritual warriors do not seek fame or recognition, do not seek respect and human praise, and do not require a title, a large salary, or a single thing from men. Their humble hearts never look for such things, because they know that their praise will one day come from God, and that His praise is better than that of a hundred million men. (See 1 Corinthians 4:5.)

Beloved, if we will have the hand of God in our day, if we will stop wicked kings in their tracks by using the awesome wisdom and cunning of the Lord, then we too must take on the nature of the poor in spirit. Humility seeks no praise, and expects no credit for service rendered. Instead, like the unprofitable servant Jesus described in Luke 17:10, the humble say, "We have simply done what was our duty to do."

Note the final statement concerning the poor wise man who delivered his city: "Yet no one remembered that same poor man." I am sure that was okay with him. The fact that he had wisdom indicates that he knew how unnecessary fame was, and how damaging it can be. How would it affect you, my friend? Desire it not, for there is no limit to the good you can do if you don't care who gets the credit.

20
God's Hand is Lifted Up

As we have seen in this study, God's hand refers mostly to His inexhaustible power to bless and to save. For example, when Isaiah says, "Behold, the Lord's hand is not shortened, that it cannot save" (59:1), he is revealing the truth that God's ability to rescue is unequalled. Jehovah's hand is exclusively His, no one else owns or controls it, and it is an expression and agent of His absolute sovereignty. Indeed, there is no situation too great for Him to handle, no stress is beyond His ability to calm, and no power is too evil and strong for Him to eradicate. This being the case, why won't He bring healing to every ill situation? Why won't He eradicate all evil with one stroke of His hand? Think about that for a moment. If the Lord set out to eradicate evil in one swift move, He would need to eradicate evil in its every form and manifestation. If He were to do that, then you and I would cease to exist. You see, even as Christians whose spirits are born again, evil is still present in our physical bodies. (See Romans 7:17-20.) Therefore the Lord is longsuffering in bringing about His judgment on evil, allowing every human being more time to repent and yield to His transforming power. But time is running out. We now live in an epoch of time that is unlike any other in history. It appears as though the "transgressors are reaching their fullness" (Daniel 8:23), and will soon bring the heavy hand of judgment upon the entire unredeemed human race. It may be that the ends of the ages are finally culminating on this generation, and that ours is the one that will see Jesus return in power and great glory! As this is very possible, we need, as never before, glowing manifestations of His mighty hand to gather in the final harvest.

His Uplifted Hand: Not Always a Blessing

While the hand of the Lord typically represents His approval, pleasure, and willingness to prosper His people, it can also represent His extreme displeasure and judgment. When God's commandments are ignored, evil enemies are sometimes unleashed, negative consequences result, and stressful incidents begin to increase both in frequency and intensity. This will occur until the rebel faces up to his wrongdoing and repents. These negative consequences first come in the form of chastisements to correct us (if allowed), and later as judgments to eliminate us (if we have hardened our hearts). In the Christian's life, hardships are to be endured and seen as forms of discipline that can train us in godliness. When God's hand of discipline is applied either directly or indirectly, it will often turn foolish people back to Him.

Most of us like to claim that the hardships we face are the result of our doing everything right, and that the persecutions come by Satan's design to stop us in our splendid progress. This line of reasoning removes the onus from us, making it possible for us to avoid any self-examination. For a few Christians, this argument may well be justified, but not for the majority of us. Most of the Christians I know do not assume this self-righteous position. Instead, they realize that, more likely than not, their own foolishness or rebellion has opened the door, creating an avenue of invasion upon which the enemy has hustled misery into their lives. Such Christians blame neither God nor the Devil for such woe, but readily admit their own weaknesses or sins.

Who's To Blame?

Fools, because of their transgression, and because of their iniquities, were afflicted. ... Then they cried out to the Lord in their trouble, and He saved them out of their distresses.
Psalm 107:17, 19

Before I was afflicted I went astray, but now I keep Your word.

Psalm 119:67

My strength fails because of my iniquity, and my bones waste away.

Psalm 31:10b

Note how Psalm 119:17 pinpoints the afflicted fool. It is because of transgression, or because he has "stepped over the line," that the fool is afflicted. God cannot receive the blame for this, not when we read how the Lord offers the believer a "secret place," and a hedge of protection throughout his or her life. Even so, the enemy regularly probes this hedge, and seeks ways to penetrate and afflict our lives.

Weak or Wicked?

I visited an old woman not long ago who was suffering horribly with arthritis in her spine. As I sat listening to the conversation she was having with a fellow minister, I heard her confess the longtime bitterness she carried toward a certain family member. This had provided the soft spot in her hedge. Through it the enemy had invaded her life and brought the classic symptom of bitterness, which is arthritis. Now I ask, is this woman wicked? Absolutely not! She is simply another weak individual who has had her spirit wounded by the thoughtless actions of someone she should have been able to trust. She is another person who doesn't know how to process the wounds of life, and Satan has taken advantage of it.

I have learned that sometimes there is a difference between a weak person and a wicked person. The weak person may have a kind heart, but lack the wisdom that is necessary for the overcoming life. A weak person can be hurt, and not know how to quell the rage they feel within. A weak person may stumble and fall, and not know how to get up again. A weak person may habitually sin, and not know how to take

189

dominion over the sin that besets their life. There is more hope for him than you may realize, for when he gets a revelation of God's grace, he eagerly reaches for it.

A wicked person, on the other hand, has not an ounce of kindness in his heart, but is deceitful and self-serving through and through. God's goodness means little to such a person; in fact, His goodness often goes unnoticed and unappreciated. The wicked, therefore, persists in his rebellion, adding sin to sin against the Day of Judgment. For this reason, I believe such a person is in line for a harsher sentence of judgment than are the weak and foolish. The Lord's wrath ultimately crashes down upon those who refuse to learn righteousness by His Word. Although God would rather we order our lives by what is written in His Word (2 Timothy 3:16), we don't always do this. Therefore judgment catches transgressors unexpectedly, and affliction in one form or another overpowers them. The prophet succinctly declared, "Your own wickedness will correct you, and your backslidings will rebuke you…" (Jeremiah 2:19). One way or the other, in time or eternity, the sinner will face his transgression and answer for it!

But to the Church, Paul wrote, "For if we would judge ourselves, we would not be judged" (1 Corinthians 11:31). The Lord truly has a better way for you and me to learn righteousness. "How can a young man cleanse his way?" asks the Psalmist. "By taking heed according to Your Word," is the reply (Psalm 119:9). But if one refuses to examine and adjust his life (its attitudes and actions) by the Word, harsh judgments from other sources will come upon him. This is never God's perfect will, but lies within the scope of His permissive will. When this happens, His desire is that the negative pressures drive us back to the righteousness that pleases Him. Paul added, "But when we are judged, we are chastened by the Lord, that we may not be condemned with the world" (11:32).

How Judgment Comes Today

There should be no doubt that God judged the world for its sin when Jesus died on the cross. Isaiah said that by oppression and judgment He was taken away. Like the scapegoat on ancient Israel's Day of Atonement, Jesus was cut off from the land of the living (Leviticus 16:22; Isaiah 53:8), and for the transgressions of the world He was stricken! When the sun went down over Jerusalem on that awesome day, God's judgment on sin had been fully executed and the claims of justice were fully satisfied. Since that day, His perfect, indisputable will is that every human life forsake sin, reject self-righteousness, and give heart, soul, mind and strength, to serve the King of kings. He wants to be done with wrath, judgment and execution. He wants everyone to be saved. He wants the world to fill up with men and women who embrace and follow the Lamb. Tragically, however, that has not happened! In spite of the efforts of the Church to evangelize and convert the world to Christianity, blind and rebellious men continue to rise up and spurn Christ's Lordship.

God has not been put off by this disappointing result, and the prophetic Scriptures clearly indicate that He set in motion a battle for the souls of men that would rage until Jesus comes in glory. This battle involves elements of both redemption and judgment. It entails outbursts of almightiness to bless and to curse; to build up and tear down; to bind and to loose! God alone knows when judgments are necessary to deal with wicked men and nations. He knows that at times the world's despots need to be removed from power, and He appoints anointed men to do it. He knows when the defiant behavior of rank sinners needs to be confronted, and the slaughter of innocents stopped. He knows when rebellion needs to be intercepted and chastised. He alone knows the full fury of His judgments! But that isn't His will for mankind. His will is that the punishment Jesus bore at the cross be sufficient for everyone! His will is that all men receive His

Son. However, scores of people continue to reject the judgment Christ endured there. They continue to reject God's sacrifice for their transgressions. They continue to snub His offer of mercy. But as far as He is concerned, man's redemption is signed, sealed and delivered through the death, burial and resurrection of Jesus Christ. What each person does with this offer is another question altogether. Yet the Redeemer's life has been laid down, the price has been paid, and the way to salvation has been opened for all who will take it for themselves by faith.

The Lord Must Yet Judge

God judges sin in both time and eternity. He judges sin directly, as in Acts 12:23, when He commissioned an angel to smite King Herod, and He judges sin indirectly, as when He steps back and allows suffering to humble a people. Because men and women continue to defy the Lord and act in concert with their spiritual father, the Devil, God must yet wield the rod of judgment. His judgments, however, come more in the form of correction and adjustment, than condemnation and complete eradication. He forever seeks to adjust a man's behavior and challenge his ideas through the hardships He allows into his life.

I view chastisement and judgment as being two different things. Chastisement is for corrective purposes, where judgment is more for the purpose of elimination. The Lord is perfectly capable of executing both. In this world of time, He doles out both corrective and eliminating punishments, but His strongest wrath on wicked humanity will not begin until the Tribulation Period and ultimately at the Great White Throne Judgment of Revelation 20. (See chapter 15.) Even so, we are seeing a form of God's judgment in many nations right now. We call these His *temporal* judgments. This is not His eternal judgment; that will come later, but they are hardships and catastrophes allowed for the purpose of bringing correction to a disobedient and rebellious people. Often when people experience temporal judgments, they are given a chance to repent and correct things that have gone awry. When God lifts His hand of protection, and the curse enters to devastate, it is often because He has disapproved of something that has been going on for a long time. The judgment released comes as a wake-up call. As we have already seen, the prophet proclaimed, "...when Your judgments are in the earth, the inhabitants of the world will learn righteousness" (Isaiah 26:9b).

Contemporary examples of His temporal judgment on individuals and families is seen whenever God lifts His hand of blessing and protection, and demonic powers are able to assail the physical, financial and mental well-being of the one(s) under judgment. I am not saying that this is always a case of God's temporal judgment (because Satan can sometimes get at people who have done nothing wrong), but many times it is. When this happens, God is trying to get somebody's attention.

Contemporary examples of God's temporal judgment on nations and larger groups of people are often seen when things like bad leadership, terrorism, war, natural disasters, decimating plagues, or financial calamity befall them for resisting His purposes. For example: Each time our own American government pressures Israel to concede land or compromise her principles before the United Nations and the Arab world, some type of disaster occurs here in America. This is why the praying remnant must remain vigilant, interceding for government leaders and those who make foreign policy decisions.

Sins That Offend the Lord
Many other sins, besides our treatment of Israel, have caused the Lord to lift His protective hand from western societies and allow temporal judgments to occur. Some major offenses are:

1. The Sexual Revolution. This multi-trillion dollar monster, fueled by a corrupt entertainment establishment, is more concerned with the financial bottom line, as well as with its ability to push liberal agendas, than it is with providing audiences with moral and ethical entertainment. This wicked scourge is a key reason hard times are rocking the West today. The entertainment industry's sick offerings are turning literally millions of Americans into moral zombies who adopt an "anything goes" mentality when faced with right or wrong choices. Moral absolutes, based in the Word of God, have been replaced by a secular relativism that is resolutely promoted by Hollywood screenwriters, directors and actors.

2. Homosexuality. For this sin God destroyed Sodom and Gomorrah. That is an undisputable fact! Being that Heaven's Judge is the same yesterday, and today, and forever (Hebrews 13:8), and that He declares: "I am the Lord, I do not change!", I would be a bit uneasy if I liked to sleep with people of my own sex. Homosexuality is against nature (Romans 1:26), and against God. This sin opens the door to a devastating curse if not repented of. The AIDS pandemic is nothing short of a scourge on the human race, a plague the gross sin of homosexuality helped to initiate. God is pained by this calamity, however, and finds no pleasure when people die with this or any other disease (Ezekiel 18:23). Even so, the prophet Isaiah declared: "But your iniquities have separated you from your God, and your sins have hidden His face from you, so that He will not hear" (59:2). As society continues embracing homosexuality as normal and acceptable, an escalation of judgment will occur in the coming days. God's protective grace will give way to Satan's cruel oppression as this rebellion is confronted. Scripture warns, "He who digs a pit will fall into it, and whoever breaks through a wall (of protection) will be bitten by a serpent" (Ecclesiastes 10:8). When men lie with men, and women with women, they dig inevitable pits of

194

destruction, tearing down with their own hands, every hedge of protection God would have placed around their lives had they honored His Word. As a master opportunist, Satan gleefully swoops into such people's lives, bringing a devastating curse!

3. <u>Abortion</u>. What can be said of a society that murders its own children for the sake of convenience, even to the tune of four million innocent lives a year? Since 1973 America has been guilty of this despicable holocaust. So have many other Western nations. If the blood of righteous Able cried to God from the ground, invoking a horrendous curse upon his murderer, what does the blood of nearly fifty million innocent babies say to the Lord? What will it cost this world in the end? It is a sad day when a nation's judges charge a man with a double homicide for killing his wife and unborn baby, and yet defend that same woman's right to abort a child if she wants to. One murder is no less offensive to God than the other, and, in the end, justice will be served! How can a nation expect to avoid God's frightening hand of fury when it persists in this kind of atrocity?

4. <u>Occultism and Sorcery</u>. Whenever someone seeks supernatural answers or power from the spiritual world, they are transgressing the law of God. Throughout the Bible it is written that men and women "should seek unto their God" when needing spiritual help and guidance, and not to wizards, mediums and spiritualists (Isaiah 8:19-22). Psalm 16:4 warns, "Their sorrows shall be multiplied who hasten after another god." Much of the agony plaguing individuals, families and societies, is the result of this very transgression. Paul taught that through (Jesus) we have access to the Father, and that *by one Spirit* we can tap supernatural help (Ephesians 2:18). Supernaturalism that doesn't find its source in Jesus Christ, or gain its access by the Holy Spirit, is both illegitimate and

criminal, and will sooner or later incur the temporal judgment of God. The Lord says to everyone who would seek supernatural assistance from other sources: "So you want to get your answers by methods and from sources I don't condone, do you? Go ahead if you must, but you'll only find a subtle and devastating curse!"

5. Radical Feminism and Witchcraft. Witchcraft in this sense does not refer to the mystic brand where a woman worships female deities, casts spells, wears a pointed hat, or mixes evil potions. The brand of witchcraft I speak of here is the kind listed in Galatians 5:20, which is a manipulative, coercing work of the fallen nature. Both men and women can operate in this kind of psychic power, making life miserable for everyone under their influence. Radical feminism reeks of this brand of witchery, seeking to feminize society, and thereby gain the upper hand. Often the women used in this way have little or no understanding of how lethal they are in the hands of the Devil. In truth, they usually don't even consider themselves to be very spiritual. But what results is devastating. The prophet Nahum describes the judgment on a society—any society—that becomes feminized: "Surely your people in your midst are women! The gates of your land are wide open for your enemies; fire shall devour the bars of your gates" (3:13). Warfare should never enter the gates of our own cities. Instead, as God's people, we are to carry the battle into the gates of our enemies! However, when effeminate leadership seizes control of a nation, a church, or a home, the enemy is able to deliver its payload of violence.

Feminism is not a sex, but a spirit. It enslaves men as well as women. The feminine spirit cloaking America's church and government leaders in recent years has allowed the nation to get in a place where it is vulnerable, having to fight Satan's work within its own gates. Remember 9-11? Because the Western church did not take seriously the work of evangelizing the Middle East following the Second World War, extreme

196

elements of Islam arose to force battle into the gates of Western nations. America, Canada, France and Britain are today facing an enormous power play by Islamic fundamentalists who are hell-bent on flying their flag over every capitol building in the West. It was good that George W. Bush forced the physical battle back into the gates of militant Muslims, but that will not produce positive results *if* the Church doesn't follow through with aggressive and sustained prayer and evangelism!

In my opinion, women are crowning jewels in God's creation. "The royal daughter is all glorious *within* the palace (of the King)" (Psalm 45:13). Women are beautiful and intelligent creatures, perfectly designed to compliment mankind—their fellow creation. Together with fathers, mothers, brothers, sisters, husbands and children, they are to worship and serve their Lord and King. But *outside* the palace, *outside* their proper place in God's kingdom, they are awkward, and not nearly so fruitful as when flowing in a God-ordained function. When men and women exchange roles in society, and when God must say, "children are their oppressors, and women rule over them," a recipe for disaster is created. (See Isaiah 3:12.) This is precisely what we are facing in Western nations today! When I speak of women keeping their proper place in society, I am not promoting oppression, but freedom. The kind of binding oppression placed on women in many countries is wrong! In societies where women are forced into subjection, the Lord is heart-broken. Actually, Jesus Christ liberates women to be all they can be for God's glory! Women should have as much right as anyone to prosper in a free society. But I do address the kind of women who constantly rise up against men, even against considerate men with legitimate authority, and seek to gain positions that do not belong to them. I am addressing those women who have a "chip on their shoulder," and generally dislike men, as well as any position in society that makes them feel inferior to men. These types of women set themselves against God. These women place themselves in harm's way by being militant and radical.

Isaiah reveals a devastating judgment on women who use their power to usurp authority and manipulate other people: "Therefore the Lord will strike with a scab the crown of the head of the daughters of Zion, and uncover their secret parts" (3:17). Cancers, hysterectomies, radiation, chemotherapy—such miseries are often the fruits of the curse befalling women because of this rampant form of witchcraft. Not every woman suffering such a plague is evil or personally responsible for what is happening to her, but the atmosphere of rebellion created by those who are guilty is affecting women everywhere! Will Judgment Day reveal how feminists cursed entire nations by their aggressive and militant witchcraft? I believe it will.

Isaiah continues: "Instead of a sweet smell there will be a stench; instead of a sash, a rope; instead of well-set hair, baldness" (3:24). Does this speak of baldness due to chemotherapy, and other forms of aggressive medical treatment? Does God's Word here speak in generalities, or is it quite specific in its descriptions?

The sin of witchcraft will incur even greater judgments in coming days. Christian women, therefore, must deliberately choose to order their lives by the Holy Scriptures, and thus find a sure place in the protection of God's grace. (See Proverbs 31:10-31; Ephesians 5:22-24, 33b; 1 Peter 3:3-6; 1 Timothy 2:9-15; 5:1-14.) From this sure place, and like lifeguards tossing life rings to those being pulled under by the churning riptides of storm-tossed seas, sisters in Christ in the last days will "hold forth the Word of Life" to a crooked and perverse generation that is sinking beneath the waves of a devastating curse.

6. <u>Political and Corporate Corruption</u>. The two often go hand-in-hand, each scratching the other's back in return

for special favors. This high-level brand of corruption often goes unnoticed by anyone but the Lord. Even if the common man knows when and where such wickedness is happening, there is very little he can do about it. The powers that be are just too strong for their opponents. Too many high-powered lawyers represent them, and too many corrupt judges are protecting them.

7. <u>The Drug Pandemic</u>. This heartbreaking scourge is fueled by a principality of sorcery that is determined to reduce western societies to a piece of bread. America's best and brightest are often the targets of such spiritual villainy, and those who might otherwise become great contributors to humanity are reduced to a rabble of insignificant losers. When a nation's social engineers allow this to happen year after year, and refuse to make the hard decisions that will stop it, judgment begins to fall. The drug pandemic is costing Americans millions of lives and billions of treasure.

8. <u>One's Treatment of Israel and the Jews</u>. God said to Abraham: "I will bless those who bless you, and curse those who curse you" (Genesis 12:3). He made this statement in context with "the great nation" he would create through Abraham. That great nation came through the loins of Abraham, Isaac and Jacob, and comprises the Jewish people. It did not come through the loins of Abraham and Ishmael! Regardless of the corruption, idolatry, and rebellion witnessed among the Jews over the centuries, God's promise still stands: "I will bless those who bless you, and curse those who curse you!" Even so, anti-Semitism rages on, and remains one of the most detestable sins in the eyes of the Lord. God alone reserves the right to decide when, where and how He will punish His backslidden Jewish people, and for an individual or a nation to make or execute their own form of judgment against Israel and/or the Jews is dangerous indeed!

For My sword shall be bathed in heaven; indeed it shall come down on Edom, and on the people of My curse, for judgment. The sword of the Lord is filled with blood.

Isaiah 34:5-6a

Edom serves as a representative of all nations hostile to Israel. Judgment first takes place in the heavens (against anti-Semitic principalities), and then it comes down to the earth. In coming days we will see such judgments intensify drastically. (See Jeremiah 10:25; Numbers 24:9; Obadiah 15.)

Let us now go to the Old Testament and examine God's hand of judgment at earlier times in history.

21
His Hand of Judgment in Scripture

Divine judgments, though terrifying, are at the same time purifying. They are necessary societal and national adjustments that can only be avoided as mankind chooses to know and serve the living God. As long as fallen humans walk the planet, judgments will occur. The time will come, however, when wickedness and judgment will be no more, and there will only be a world wherein dwells righteousness.

For evildoers shall be cut off; but those who wait on the Lord, they shall inherit the earth. For yet a little while and the wicked shall be no more; indeed, you will look carefully for his place, but it shall be no more. But the meek shall inherit the earth, and shall delight themselves in the abundance of peace.

Psalm 37:9-11

God's Hand in Judgment on Egypt

To understand God's future hand in judging wickedness, it helps to examine His judgments of the past. Let us pull from a few examples where "the hand of the Lord" was involved in bringing correction or destruction to sinful nations long ago.

*Then the Lord said to Moses, Go in to Pharaoh and tell him, Thus says the Lord God of the Hebrews: "Let My people go, that they may serve Me. For if you refuse to let them go, and still hold them, behold, **the hand of the Lord** will be on your cattle in the field, on the horses, on the donkeys, on the camels, on the oxen, and on the sheep—a vary severe pestilence.*

Exodus 9:1-3

When one reads the full account of Israel's deliverance from Egypt, he discovers that God was indeed a man of His word. Resulting from Pharaoh's stubborn refusal to release Israel, a great pestilence swept through Egypt's livestock as God's hand of judgment turned against them. In fact, the hand of God's fury continued to fall on the land of Egypt until Pharaoh let the people go.

In coming days we will see the hand of God fall on defiant despots and nations that close their doors to the gospel. I realize that prophetic Scriptures show a time coming when the Antichrist will gain great power and influence over nations, but until that time arrives, rulers and their governments that think they have things sewed up will find that they haven't, and God will move awesome forces against them, both natural and spiritual, in order to free their peoples to hear and respond to the gospel.

Islam is one of those enemies with which God is presently dealing. Many Islamic rulers, both secular and religious, as well as the radicals who follow their lead, have their sights set on world domination. Many Muslim zealots claim that the Islamic flag will be flying over all world capitol buildings by the middle of the twenty-first century. If the true Church of Jesus Christ does not wake up and take prayer and spiritual warfare more seriously than it has, this extreme goal could be realized in more nations than we care to admit. And what would a world under Islamic rule look like? Just look across the oceans at the untold millions of people who sit beneath Islam's oppressive paw. Consider those who are denied the right to hear the gospel preached with power. God has taken Islam's threats as a personal challenge. He will get the gospel into those nations in these last days, even if He has to eliminate every defiant despot in the process. And please don't be deceived: the God of the Christian and the god of the Muslim are not the same God. [14] Allah is nothing more than a major ruling prince in heavenly places who resists Christ's claim to earth's billions.

Before I say more about God's judgment on heathen nations, let us examine a few Scriptures that reveal that God's hand is sometimes set against His own rebellious people, Israel.

God's Hand in Judgment on Rebellious Israel

*If you do not obey the voice of the Lord, but rebel against the commandment of the Lord, then **the hand of the Lord** will be against you.*

1 Samuel 12:15

*Wherever they went out [to battle], **the hand of the Lord** was against them for calamity, as the Lord had said, and as the Lord had sworn to them. And they were greatly distressed.*

Judges 2:15

Following the death of Joshua, the children of Israel abandoned their commitment to the Lord, and began worshipping the gods of the nations around them. And again, as a man of His word, the Lord put His hand against them. To go into battle is horrible enough as it is, but to face battle and discover that God has put His own hand against you must be terrifying.

As with nations, so with individuals—especially those who know better than to turn away from the living God. Such people have a form of pride that says, "I can go my own way! I can do as I please! I can worship what, how and when I see fit!" Against this arrogance and rebellion, the strong hand of God will eventually come. Whether against full-blown secularism, false religion, witchcraft, or some other form of devious spiritual activity, God's power will ultimately be unleashed. In reality, the worship of anyone or anything other than the Lord is the worship of demons (1 Corinthians 10:20). When people offer their time, money, and worship to anyone other than the Father and His Son, they please the demonic realm, and incur God's sore displeasure. Judgment will be terrifying for those who follow false ways and who seek mediums, wizards, and other spirits for help and information! "Their sorrows shall be multiplied who hasten after another god" (Psalm 16:4). People like these actually seek the dead on behalf of the living when they turn to false ways (Isaiah 8:19). At the height of rebellion, their deception is compounded, and they bring upon themselves the judgment written:

> *Then they will look to the earth (for answers), and see trouble and darkness, gloom of anguish; and they will be driven into (more) darkness.*
>
> Isaiah 8:22

God's Hand in Judgment on the Philistines

Among the many enemies Israel faced throughout the centuries, the Philistines were probably the most persistent. The hand of the Lord was raised against these people more than any other people that ever existed. When the Philistines captured the Ark of the Covenant, carrying it to the capitol city of Ashdod, the Lord really got angry!

> *But **the hand of the Lord** was heavy upon the people of Ashdod, and He ravished them and struck them with tumors, both Ashdod and its territory*
>
> 1 Samuel 5:6

Every true believer today, in a sense, is an ark of the Covenant. The Lord's presence no longer abides in one elaborate box carried about on the shoulders of priests, but abides in millions of born again men and women who love and serve Jesus Christ. One of the mysteries hidden in past ages was that God would one day dwell within the hearts of His people. As a result of Jesus' death, magnificent resurrection, and glorious ascension, the Holy Spirit is now given to indwell every believer. With God inside, each Christian becomes a member of a "holy priesthood," commissioned to offer up spiritual sacrifices to God (1 Peter 2:5; Revelation 5:10; Hebrews 13:15). As the Lord jealously watched over the former ark in Old Covenant times, He also watches over each ark (believer) in New Covenant times. We are precious in His eyes.

When the magistrates of nations persecute and imprison God-filled Christian people, it won't be long before those magistrates will feel the hand of the Lord against them. They may not know what is happening, but their violence against His people incurs God's anger. All kinds of traumatic occurrences befall these people until they either die or repent, worshiping the One they vicariously persecuted as they tormented His people.

*So the Philistines were subdued, and they did not come anymore into the territory of Israel. And **the hand of the Lord** was against the Philistines all the days of Samuel.*
1 Samuel 7:13

God's Hand in Judgment on David

Remove Your plague from me; I am consumed by the blow of Your hand.
Psalm 39:10

I am not sure what plagued David, causing him to feel that God's hand of judgment was upon him, but I know whatever it was, he repented and experienced restoration and healing. It must be dreadful to feel that the blow of God's hand is consuming you. If you have any question, turn your face to the wall and seek the Lord for His wisdom. He will let you know what is wrong. Then repent with all of your heart! It may be that God hasn't put His hand against you at all, but something amiss in your life has released a demonic flood that must be identified and turned back! Examine Psalm 107 with me to see what I mean:

Fools, because of their transgression, and because of their iniquities, are afflicted.
Vs. 17

Obedience and righteous conduct never bring affliction on the children of God, but disobedience and rebellion do! Satan finds legal ground to touch our lives when we persist in sin. But even then there is deliverance when we repent and call out to God.

Then they cried out to the Lord in their trouble, and He saved them out of their distresses. He sent His word and healed them, and delivered them from their destructions.
Vs. 19-20

When we slip over into sin, the prince of this world finds occasion against us. "Before I was afflicted," the Psalmist wrote, "I went astray" (Psalm 119:67a). On the other hand, Jesus could confidently say, "The prince of this world cometh, and hath nothing in Me" (John 14:30). Jesus was untouchable because He was diligent to keep Himself in His Father's perfect will. But you and I are more prone to miss it along the way. When this happens, we have a way back! When we cry out to God in repentance, He hears and sends *His word* to restore and heal us. However, we must heed that word as it comes! "...But now I keep Your Word" (119:67b). The first thing the Word will do is address our sin—the thing that got us into

206

trouble in the first place. If we don't respond with integrity before Him, the healing power of His Word will pass us by. There are many people who stubbornly hold to things that jeopardize their welfare. Until they let go of certain things, there will be no hope of God's healing power.

For example: Resentment and bitterness are deadly killers when lodged in the heart of the one who has them. Regardless of how much an offended person seeks healing and deliverance, God's power will not show up if their hatred remains. They must forgive, and drop the right to remain angry. They must release the one who hurt them, and toss away the crutch that lets everyone know that they're emotionally crippled. They must pardon the offender, and come out of the self-made refuge where they think they won't be hurt anymore. And they must grant clemency; throwing away the axe they want to grind—the weapon they would like to bury between the shoulder blades of the one who offended them. If they fail to do this, Satan will continue to have a heyday in their lives!

Another example of holding to things that jeopardize our welfare has to do with the possession of wrong things. Affliction may be in your life because you brought something home that invites demonic activity. Deuteronomy charges us, "Neither shall you bring an abomination into your house, lest you be doomed to destruction like it" (7:26).

Years ago we had friends with a dynamic and fruitful deliverance ministry. One day, a lady came to their house who was dying of cancer. During pre-deliverance counseling they learned that she had several little Buddha's in her house, idols she had purchased while traveling throughout Southeast Asia. Demons often attach themselves to items like these, because such things have been used in the worship of false gods. When accursed things enter your home, certain demons accompany them, seeking opportunity to bring harm to your entire family. If leprosy (mildew, mold, or dry rot) could literally get in the walls of Jewish homes (Leviticus 14:33-53), doesn't it stand to reason that other diseases can also get into people's houses? I believe that leprosy in the walls of some Israelite homes symbolized the fact that evil spirits and the diseases they carry seek opportunities to move in with us and bring destruction. Leprosy in the walls of Jewish homes was not limited to a purely natural disorder, but was also intricately related to an existing spiritual disorder. Why else would a priest have to go and declare the house unclean, and then take the appropriate measures and rid it of the plague? Why else would he have to offer sacrifices, and make atonement before health could return? The possession of false gods and occult paraphernalia makes it very possible for demons of disease and turmoil to enter a home and bring destruction to every facet of one's life. Unreasonable amounts of sickness can occur, family disputes and alienation can take place, financial difficulties can spring forth, and mental and emotional health can be severely assaulted.

Encouraged by her promise to destroy the Buddha's once she returned home, our friends cast several strong demons from the lady. One of them identified itself as Cancer, and came out whining and screaming bloody murder! When it left, all symptoms of the disease left with it. A healthy color returned to her face as strength returned to her body. You would think that this lady's gratefulness would cause her to do whatever she was told to do by her deliverers. But this story has a sad ending.

When the lady returned home, healed, delivered and feeling much better, she allowed the Devil to get to her mind. She looked at her idols, appreciating the exquisite craftsmanship that went into each of them, and couldn't reconcile herself with their destruction. Recalling how much money they cost, she reasoned that their destruction would be a huge waste. So she decided to keep them. In about six months the cancer returned to her body, and she died not long afterwards. I believe that the cancer never left the walls of her home, but was waiting for her disobedience to run out of time.

Those who want God's blessing, but who want to remain a *little* disobedient at the same time, are like children who dance as close to a roaring fire as possible, seeing how close they can get without getting burned. In this lady's case, the flames reached out and engulfed her!

God's Hand in Judgment on a Sorcerer

*And now, indeed, **the hand of the Lord** is upon you, and you shall be blind, not seeing the sun for a time. And immediately a dark mist fell on him, and he went around seeking someone to lead him by the hand.*

Acts 13:11

Elymas was a strong and influential sorcerer in the city of Paphos. The story hints that he was a manipulative man, exercising power over people in low and high places alike. When he attempted to interfere with Paul's ministry to the proconsul of Paphos, the apostle would not have it for a moment. He swiftly pronounced a temporal judgment on the warlock, declaring that the hand of God was on him! Immediately Elymas lost his sight. What amazes me is that Paul wielded such authority with God; that his words carried that kind of power. To think that the Lord would release His own strong hand of judgment based on the prophetic declaration of His faithful servant is sobering. What authority is available to the Church of Jesus Christ today?

Years ago, when Bishop Benson Idahosa was alive and ministering in Nigeria, West Africa, he used this kind of authority when dealing with a program director that stubbornly refused to sell him airtime on a government operated television station. After politely asking for a time slot on at least two different occasions, and continually experiencing a searing denial, Idahosa boldly declared: "Alright lady, but it will cost you your job!" As he turned to leave her office, he did so amidst a barrage of curse words, but that didn't keep his words from coming to pass. Within the month the lady was fired, and a much more gracious program director was hired who eagerly sold Idahosa the time he needed to preach the gospel to Nigeria's millions. In the days to come, we will again see certain servants of the Most High wield this kind of spiritual authority. The strong hand of the Lord will be fearsome indeed!

Into the Hands of an Angry God

For **_in the hand of the Lord_** there is a cup, and the wine is red; it is fully mixed, and He pours it out; surely its dregs shall all the wicked of the earth drain and drink down.
Psalm 75:8

Now the Egyptians are men, and not God; and their horses are flesh, and not spirit. When the Lord stretches out **_His hand_**, both he who helps will fall, and he who is helped will fall down; they all will perish together
Isaiah 31:3

Son of man, when a land sins against Me by persistent unfaithfulness, I will stretch out **_My hand_** against it; I will cut off its supply of bread, send famine on it, and cut off man and beast from it.
Ezekiel 14:13

Behold, therefore, I stretched out **_My hand_** against you, diminished your allotment, and gave you up to the will of those who hate you, the daughters of the Philistines, who were ashamed of your lewd behavior.
Ezekiel 16:27

As I read these verses from the Word of God, I shudder

210

to think how His hand will soon be turned on the nations that deny His Lordship and rule. The cup His hand now holds is indeed full of the deep red wine of His fury, and both wicked men and nations will soon be forced to drink it down.

The verse in Ezekiel 16:27 bothers me for many Western nations. Our lewd behavior, our pornography, prostitution, homosexuality, drug addictions and gross feminism, make our enemies blush when they look our way. No wonder Muslims call America "The Great Satan." No wonder they want to rid the world of the kind of people they see on TV shows, in Hollywood movies, and in the glossy advertisements of worldly magazines. They think all Americans live like that. The sad thing is that we are not ashamed! Our politicians think it doesn't matter. Our entertainers are proud of their sick and putrid offerings from the pit. Our teachers and educators are dumber than Hell itself! In time or eternity, a fearful judgment is coming on all ungodly people!

"Yeah, give it to them, brother!" you might applaud. But what of God's people? What of the giddy, "live-as-I-please" brand of Christians we see today? They lounge in our church buildings on Sunday mornings, yet live for themselves all other mornings of the week? Should they fear God's hand? Consider these sobering words:

*For if we sin willfully after we have received a knowledge of the truth, there no longer remains a sacrifice for sins, but a certain fearful expectation of judgment, and fiery indignation which shall devour the adversaries...For we know Him who said, "Vengeance is Mine, I will repay," says the Lord. And again. "The Lord will judge His people." It is a fearful thing to fall **into the hands** of the living God.*
Hebrews 10:26-27, 30-31

Notice that in these verses the Lord connects judgment

211

to "His people." Therefore, each of us should check closely to see if we are truly what we claim to be. (See 2 Corinthians 13:5.) Peter understood the danger, and warned: "For the time has come for judgment to begin at the house of God" (1 Peter 4:17).

Should a stern form of judgment come to North American congregations next Sunday morning—the kind that befell the church in Jerusalem when Ananias and Sapphira dropped dead for lying to the Holy Spirit—how would we fare? How many people in the pews near you would be carried out on stretchers? How many funerals would your pastor have to preach the following week? We yearn for the fire of God's power and glory, but are we really prepared for it? Are we ready for its purging work? Remember, the God to whom we cry out for mighty outpourings, is also a consuming fire! As living fire, He displays a raging zeal for holiness and a pure hatred for sin. Before He can release the level of power we long for, He must judge and prepare us for life at that higher level. Isaiah asked, "Who among us shall dwell with the devouring fire? Who among us shall dwell with everlasting burnings?" (33:14). Only Christians with clean hands and pure hearts will be able to stand in the presence of the Consuming Fire.

Peter continues: "If judgment begins with us, what will be the end of those who do not obey the gospel of God?" He then asks, "If the righteous one is scarcely saved, where will the ungodly and the sinner appear?" (1Peter 4:17-18). This question is terrifying, isn't it! Every human being will one day fall into the hands of the righteous Judge, some for mercy and others for damnation. Scripture reveals that He will appear as loving Father to a small minority, but to the most He will manifest Himself as terrifying Judge!

The Lord God, the righteous Judge of Heaven and earth, has not changed colors. The robe in which He now appears carries authority in Heaven's High Court. As the One

212

ordained by the Godhead to execute vengeance on evildoers; as the One ordained to be the Judge of the living and the dead, Jesus will soon ascend the Judgment Bench! While He possesses infinite mercy for those who trust and reach out to Him, He will be amazingly stern with those who spurned His offers of grace and forgiveness while they lived on earth.

Are You Weak or Wicked?

As we considered earlier, the Lord alone knows the difference between a weak person and a wicked one. Which one do you suppose you are? When we die, God deals with us according to His own infinite understanding of our heart and life, and how we chose to relate to Jesus. Some people falter and sin throughout their sojourn here because they were weak, and somehow have failed to access God's power to overcome the sin and evil in their lives. Punishment will come to these just as it will to the violently wicked; only their punishment won't be as severe. But those who enjoy their wickedness actually pull at sin "as if with a cart rope" (Isaiah 5:18). Judgment on these individuals will be horrifying to say the least. According to Isaiah 14:15, the pit of Hades has various depths and recesses. The verse speaks of the "lowest depths," and the "inmost recesses." (See also Proverbs 9:18; 7:27.) The inmost recesses of Hades are reserved for those who have found the greatest pleasure in wickedness.

22

His Frightening Hand on the Nations

*Awake, awake! Stand up, O Jerusalem, you who have drunk **at the hand of the Lord** the cup of His fury...*
Isaiah 51:17

It is a fearful thing to drink from the cup of God's fury, and yet the wicked have been doing so since God's first covenants with mankind. First, Noah's generation drank from this cup, being totally annihilated by the great flood. A few generations later, Egypt's Pharaoh and his entire army felt the blow of His hand, and were drowned in the midst of the sea. Other heathen nations in history were also forced to drink the cup of God's fury. On one night alone, the Angel of the Lord smote 185,000 Assyrian soldiers who had gathered to destroy Judah. (See 2 Kings 19:35.)

The fury of God's judgment has not been limited to heathen nations, but has also befallen evil and backslidden people of His own nation. Take Korah's mutiny for example. The Lord was so offended by Korah, and all those who joined his rebellion, that He caused the earth to open up and swallow them whole! (See Numbers 16.) Time and again God allowed His judgment to come upon the backslidden nation in an attempt to turn their hearts back to Him.

Circumcise yourselves to the Lord, and take away the foreskins of your hearts, you men of Judah and inhabitants of Jerusalem, lest My fury come forth like fire, and burn so that no one can quench it, because of the evil of your doings.
Jeremiah 4:4

Disobedience has always been a major reason for judgment on Israel. The Lord's judgments should correct His

215

people and turn them back to Him, but they don't always do that.

> *Therefore He has poured on him the fury of His anger and the strength of battle; it has set him on fire all around, yet he did not know; and it burned him, yet he did not take it to heart.*   Isaiah 42:25

Fury defined means: "Violent anger; wild rage."[15] Bible dictionaries simply define it as heat—the heat of His anger unleashed on rampant evil and sin.

Could the gentle Lamb of God, the merciful Father, and the consoling Holy Spirit, yet be capable of raising a furious hand against individuals and nations that persist in sin? Please read the remainder of this chapter sitting down.

Throughout the history of mankind, God has poured out His fury, in one form or another, on wicked individuals and nations, and He will continue to do so. Certain kinds of sin, as well as the sinners who commit them, must periodically slam headlong into the wall of judgment or they will spread and fill the earth. God will not allow this to happen, and so He brings judgment to retard gross sin's rapid growth in mankind.

Judgment comes in the form of war, pestilence and famine. It shows itself through natural disasters, droughts, and in the spiritual and physical captivity of a nation's children. (See Deuteronomy 28.)

God also allows persecution as a form of judgment on His own straying people. Some Christians are persecuted for being faithful to the Lord and His Word; but many are persecuted because they are unfaithful. It requires maturity to know the difference.

If the Lord judges His own people, we know He judges the wicked as well. Often, after God uses the wicked in judgment on his own people, He destroys them! See what He

216

told Israel:

See, I have taken out of your hand the cup of trembling,
the dregs of the cup of My fury; you shall no longer drink it.
But I will put it into the hand of those who afflict you...
Isaiah 51:22b-23a

The Lord used Babylon to persecute and enslave rebellious Israel, but when His judgment came around to Babylon, He destroyed it.

Throughout her history, Israel has tasted both God's goodness and His wrath. But so have other nations. His own perfect knowledge and impeccable judgment determine when a nation receives the one or the other. The twenty first century will be no different than past pivotal centuries. The only difference may lie in the intensity of the judgment executed. Nations judged harshly in past centuries may seem as though they received a mere slap on the wrist when compared with the severity of the judgments to come. Remember, we are at the end of the age, and everything is escalating and intensifying.

One critical signpost that will warn the righteous of when a judgment may befall a nation is seen in its treatment of Israel.

Pour out Your fury on the Gentiles who do not know
You, and on the families who do not call on Your name; for
they have eaten up Jacob, devoured him and consumed him,
and made his dwelling place desolate.
Jeremiah 10:25

For any nation, no time is a good time to oppose Zion. Even so, all nations will do so in the near future. To oppose the nation of Israel will be dangerous indeed, and the hand of the Lord will be poised to strike such nations with a severe judgment! We must, therefore, be in constant and earnest prayer for our leaders. Their decisions regarding Israel and the Church will have drastic ramifications, affecting us all. Just imagine the enormity of His judgment when all nations on earth turn against the Jews in the land of promise. (See Zechariah 12:3, 9; 14:2; Revelation 19:19.) *Apocalypse* is not a strong enough term to describe the disastrous end time scene that unfolds.

The prophet Zechariah had some fearful things to say about God's fury as it relates to the city, Jerusalem.

Thus says the Lord of hosts: "I am zealous for Zion with great zeal; with great fervor I am zealous for her."
Zechariah 8:2

The literal rendering of this verse shows that God is *jealous* for Jerusalem with great fervor, "heat or rage!" This is anything but a passive response to the unauthorized claim to His holy city by the nations of the world. As "a cup of trembling,"[16] and, "a burdensome stone," [17] Jerusalem seems to be at the center of world focus, with everybody and their brother feeling obligated to offer advice on how the Jews should settle their differences with the surrounding nations. While the nations are offering only provisional answers to Mid Eastern problems, God is taking His own counsel on what to do with Jerusalem. We can be sure that His own counsel is perfectly in line with His prophetic purposes for the nation. Regardless of the outcry from militant Muslims, the bias of world leaders, and even the self-focused agenda of the Jewish people themselves, God will keep His promise to Abraham— not because of the Jews, but in spite of them! And be assured of this: Somewhere in the near future, there is an appointment with His vengeance that will melt wicked hearts in every nation!

Wail, for the day of the Lord is at hand! It will come
as destruction from the Almighty. Behold, the day of the Lord
comes. Cruel, [with fury and burning anger].

Isaiah 13:6, 9

At the present time the Lord is withholding His strong
hand of fury, not willing to unleash it against His adversaries
until the appointed time. But the day is coming when He will
no longer suppress His fury, but will release it on all those
who withstand His purposes for the world. This coming
tumultuous time is known as The Tribulation Period, or The
Great Tribulation. It will be a fast-moving and hair-raising
interval of several years when the seven seals are broken, the
seven trumpets sound, and the seven bowls of wrath are poured
out on the nations. These will be such horrendous years that
Jesus was impressed to say, "unless those days were shortened,
no flesh would be saved!" (Matthew 24:22). However, because
of His faithfulness to fulfill prophecy and restore all things,
the Lord will vanquish His foes on the bloody fields of
Megiddo, and "suddenly come to His temple" (Malachi 3:1).
He will establish Jerusalem as His Millennial throne. Jesus
says through Zechariah, "I will return to Zion, and dwell in
the midst of Jerusalem" (8:3a). As the centerpiece of the
nations, Jerusalem shall be called the City of Truth, the
Mountain of the Lord of hosts, the Holy Mountain" (8:3b).
Because He who is the Truth established it and will again
reign there, Jerusalem is called the City of Truth.

Who will Judge the Nations?

In the first six verses of Isaiah's sixty-third chapter,
an interesting conversation is recorded. The Father asks the
Spirit, some angels, or perhaps the approaching Son:

Who is this who comes from Edom, with dyed garments from Bozrah, this One who is glorious in His apparel, traveling in the greatness of His strength?

The Son arrives to answer Him:
I who speak in righteousness, mighty to save!

The Father then asks:

Why is your apparel red, and your garments like one who treads in the winepress?

The Son answers:

I have trodden the winepress alone, and from the peoples no one was with Me. For I have trodden them in my anger, and trampled them in My fury; their blood is sprinkled upon My garment, and I have stained all My robes. For the day of vengeance is in My heart, and the year of My redeemed has come.

As if that is not enough, the Son continues:

I looked, but there was no one to help, and I wondered that there was no one to uphold; therefore My own arm brought salvation for me; and My own fury, it sustained Me.

Whoa! Jesus' own fury sustains Him in judgment. Something must carry Him through it.
He then concludes:

I have trodden down the peoples in My anger, made them drunk in My fury, and brought down their strength to the earth.

These powerful words will one day tumble from the mouth of the blood-sprayed Redeemer/Judge. The Day of vengeance is in His heart, but only because of His passionate desire to embrace His redeemed. Jesus knows that He will only take His espoused in marriage after executing the Judgment foretold in the prophetic Scriptures. For two thousand years He has been deprived of the level of fellowship with His fairest that He desires and deserves. Not until after Resurrection Day, and the fierce Battle of Armageddon, will the saints be able to enter into the full sanctification promised (1 Corinthians 15:50-54; 1 John 3:1-2). And so today, Jesus is eager to be done with evil. Today He is eager to consummate this age so that the earth may move into that blessed condition "wherein dwells righteousness" (2 Peter 3:13).

As we have seen, the above conversation between the Father and the Son portends one that will occur in the aftermath of the devastating judgment of the last day. In this text, Edom, and its capital city, Bozrah, represent the entire world—its many political and financial systems, as well as its godless hordes gathered in a valley called, in the Hebrew tongue, "Megiddo."

Jesus *Himself* will "tread the winepress of the fierceness and wrath of Almighty God" (Revelation 19:15). No one is qualified to help Him; no one else has earned this inglorious distinction. What a dreadful day it will be when He whose eyes are a flame of fire descends to earth with a sharp two-edged sword proceeding from His mouth, and a rod of iron clenched firmly in His fist!

The grapes He tramples in the winepress of God's fierceness and wrath will be all those who are clustered on the vine of the earth. (See Revelation 14:17-20.) This vine does not refer to the Vine of God (the Church), but rather the complex world system that has shunned the day of grace. Its people will be *fully ripened* by sin, and totally worthy of the furious judgment being unleashed. This squares up with what the prophet Daniel wrote, when he foretold a time when "the transgressors [will reach] their fullness" (8:23). When this happens it won't be long before the Lord will descend in power, as Irresistible Battle Champion, to tread the winepress of God's wrath and fury! Sheer terror and madness of heart will seize the godless on that day, and in a frenzied, demonic rage, will incite many godless nations to battle the Lord! A mental image of this scene alone should cause us to tremble in our boots! Indeed, everyone on earth at the time of Christ's return, who has not made Him the Lord and Savior of their lives, will be thrown into the winepress of God's dealings. The blood of malicious world armies, representing rebellious end time humanity, will spurt on and splatter the garments of the Lord when He comes to rule the earth with a rod of iron! That is why the Father will ask Him on that fateful day, "Why is Your apparel red, and Your garments like one who treads the winepress?"

Clothed With Vengeance, Clad With Zeal!

*For He put on righteousness as a breastplate, and a helmet of salvation on His head; He put on the garments of vengeance for clothing, and was clad with zeal as a cloak. According to their deeds, accordingly He will repay, **fury to His adversaries**, recompense to His enemies; the coastlands He will fully repay.*

Isaiah 59:17-18, Author's emphasis

The prophet spoke of the day when the Messiah, clad in vengeance and cloaked in zeal, will recompense fury to His adversaries. Adversaries are "all those who set themselves *adversely* to His purposes." Indeed, the Scriptures are sated with both verses and passages telling of these coming days of judgment. "Great fear will seize hypocrites and sinners," wrote the Revelators, "and they will cry for the mountains and rocks

222

to fall on them and hide them from the face of Him who sits on the throne, and from the wrath of the Lamb!" (See Isaiah 33:14 and Revelation 6:15-17.) The prophet, Nahum, spoke of His fury being poured out like fire (1:6).

A flue fire raged out of control at the bottom of our chimney one cold winter night. The door at the bottom of the flue was in the basement, and so I went with a little square-nosed shovel and a metal bucket to scoop out the boiling, burning, blazing creosote. After several scoops, my bucket was a flaming, smoking cauldron, which I quickly carried up the basement steps and out into the cold night air. Once I was a safe distance from the house, I literally poured fire out like water. I would have hated to be on the receiving end of that flow! What did the Sodomites see as fire and brimstone plummeted from Heaven to obliterate their evil cities? How will the coming furious judgments of God appear to people who have spurned His authority and rejected His Son?

Final Judgment

As frightening as God's fury poured out at Armageddon will be, I think nothing will compare with the panic that will surround the Great White Throne Judgment. The Bible says that on that Day, the face of Him who sits on that Throne will be so terrifying, the earth and heaven will flee away (Revelation 20:11). So horrible will that Day be, that the wicked dead—their ashes or dust resurrected from the ground or the oceans' depths, and their spirits from the pits of Hades—will gnash with their teeth in utter and complete terror, rage and insanity!

Each human soul who appears at this Judgment Bar will be judged according to his works. But the sum total of all he did wrong in life will pale in light of the sin of rejecting Jesus. By refusing the Lord's claim to his life, each doomed soul will learn that his or her name was not recorded in the Lamb's Book of Life, and that whoever's name is not recorded therein must be cast into the lake of fire! (See Revelation 20:15.)

Where will you appear on that Day, my friend? Will you be rejoicing in the presence of King Jesus, along with the millions from the ages who were washed in His precious blood, or will you be standing in line, awaiting your appointment with the fury of God? You must settle that question in this life, and not after you die. The sooner you answer that question, the better off you'll be. Postpone it another day and you may find you've waited too long. Death could come for you before the day is finished, and then what will you do?

Thomas A'Kempis wrote, "Ah, fool, why do you think to live long when you have not one day that is safe? How many have been deceived and then suddenly snatched from the body? If today you are not prepared to die, then how will you be tomorrow? Blessed is he that always has the hour of his death before his eyes, and daily prepares his heart to be with God. If at any time you have seen another man die, remember, you must also pass this same way."

Scripture says:

Seek the Lord while He may be found, call upon Him while He is near.
Isaiah 55:6

If you read these words as a non-Christian, the working of the Holy Spirit may be accelerating your heart rate. This is a signal that He wants you to make peace with God by embracing Jesus in all His fullness. Please don't ignore this inner signal.

Behold, now is the accepted time; behold, now is the day of salvation.
2 Corinthians 6:2b

Friend, Jesus Christ will never be more willing to save you than He is right now. What will you do with His offer of salvation? Will you do like so many others, and put it off till a more convenient time? Some men put it off indefinitely, thinking they will accept the Lord only as they approach their final days. Others count on a deathbed experience similar to the one experienced by the thief on the cross. In his dying moments the condemned man embraced the King and was saved. But I find that men generally die as they have lived. If they have trained their hearts to reject Christ while they are young and robust, they will discover their hearts are yet locked in a frozen sway as the day of death approaches. One cannot unite with Jesus Christ just because he mentally decides to. The grace to be saved must be present or the prayer of repentance will go unheard. It is best to embrace the Lord when He is near, when His Spirit is present and beckoning. Nothing guarantees that He will come close to you as you approach the inevitable portal called death.

Again, if as you read these words, your heart is thumping a little harder than usual, it is probably the Holy Spirit confirming these truths to your heart. Don't ignore this, God is reaching out to you now. Embrace Him! If you are ready to make Jesus Christ the Lord of your life, then pray this simple prayer from the bottom of your heart:

Lord Jesus Christ, I come to you as a hell-bound sinner, recognizing my need of salvation. I cannot do it on my own, Lord, and therefore gladly and eagerly submit to the righteousness that comes through faith in You alone.

On the Cross You died for me. You shed Your blood to redeem and save me from my sin and from the eternal judgment I deserve. You were buried dead, but on the third day You rose again for my

justification. Thank You, Jesus, for doing this for me.

I now end my prayer by asking You to come into my heart and make me a new creation. I repent for my sins—and for all my rebellion. Though my sins are many, remove them far from me, and wash me clean.

Jesus, I take You now as the Savior and Lord of my life. With Your good Spirit to lead me, and Your living Word to teach me how I should live, I will follow You all the days of my life.

In Your name I pray, Amen.

In Closing

At the outset of this book, I said that I could not offer an exhaustive study of the subject, *The Hand of the Lord.* I know that is still the case. However, I trust that you have been inspired to pursue the Lord and seek His face as never before. Seek His face that you might discern His will for your life. Discern His will that you might walk in His power. Walk in power that you might demonstrate His kingdom. Demonstrate His kingdom so that men will believe the trueness of the gospel you preach. Preach the gospel so that men will find hope in a fallen and dying world.

Beloved, be sure to humble yourself under God's mighty hand, and *never* allow pride to direct your steps. Remember, the proud get nowhere with God! If you will walk in humility and meekness, He will exalt you to both know His will and experience His power in the coming days. Therefore take *every* opportunity to humble yourself under

His hand and enjoy a steady flow of His grace as you pursue His purpose for your life.

I leave you with a heartwarming picture of God's mighty hand after all has been said and done in this world of pain and suffering. This will be the end of darkness, the end of pride, the end of tyranny. It will be the time of triumph after travail, and the time of the glorious rising of the enduring city.

And it will be said in that day: "Behold, this is our God; we have waited for Him, and He will save us. This is the Lord; we have waited for Him; we will rejoice and be glad in His salvation." For on this mountain the hand of the Lord will rest... Isaiah 25:9-10

As busy as God's hand is today, blessing us, empowering us, and, yes, even releasing His fury on gross iniquity and injustice, I like best what I read of His hand and it's final destination. *For the hand of Jehovah shall rest in this mountain, Jerusalem.* I rejoice to know that one day every enemy of God's desire will be removed, and our gracious, benevolent Lord will be able to settle down and enjoy everything that creation was meant to be. His will be an experience of absolute light, peace and unspeakable joy—and so will ours! May the hand of our great God soon find its resting place, its refuge and delight, in the city of the great King! Amen.

NOTES

1. Some major hindrances to the release of God's power in healing, deliverance and the flow of miracles, are the counter spiritual forces of unbelief (Mark 6:5-6), religious reasoning and skepticism (Luke 5:17-22), criticism and judgment (Mark 3:1-6; Luke 3:1-6; 13:10-17), resentment and the failure to forgive (Mark 11:25); Legalism (Galatians 3:5), jealousy and envy (John 12:19; Matthew 27:12, 17-18), lack of a repentant heart (Matthew 13:15), failure to follow instructions (2 Kings 5:9-14; Luke 17:12-14), too much busyness (Luke 10:38-42), and hypocrisy (Luke 12:1).

2. Some time between the ministries of Zerubbabel and Ezra, a great lady named Esther and her uncle, Mordecai, saved the Jewish nation from a conspiracy to kill all Jews. The plan was devised by an evil Persian prince named Haman—a master manipulator. Had Esther and Mordecai not acted wisely by seeking the Lord when they learned of the plot, there would have been no remnant of exiles to return to Israel with Ezra or Nehemiah, and all those who had gone earlier with Zerubbabel would have been hounded and exterminated.

Everyone has a crucial role in the overall purposes of God on earth, and regardless of the generation in which one lives, he is as important to God's plan as anyone who has lived. But one must give himself to God's plan. Esther's courage saved the Jewish nation; your courage may save many people from Hades' eternal torment, both from your generation, as well as from the generations yet unborn.

3. Thomas Boston, *The Art of Man-Fishing,* Baker Book House, Grand Rapids, Mich., 1977, p. 25.

4. As a pastor, it breaks my heart to watch as some Christians wander from one thing to another, forever looking for something to do that might bring them a sense of fulfillment and happiness. Often, these dear ones fail to recognize (or accept) the gifting and skill they do possess, and therefore struggle to operate in areas of ministry that, to them, should be off limits.

Have you ever had to endure an hour of teaching by someone who lacks the teaching anointing? It is a horrible experience. Or have you ever had to sit and listen to someone sing a special in your church who has no anointing for song? Rather than be blessed by their offering, you grimace and feel embarrassment for them.

Beloved, be wise enough to learn what your strengths are, and humble enough to accept what they are not. Be tough enough on yourself to avoid moving into areas of ministry you are not gifted for. If you have any doubts about this, ask your leaders and friends who are themselves submitted to legitimate leadership, and beg them to be honest with you. There are things we all wish we had the talent to do, but are we humble enough to accept it when we don't have the talent? Don't we know that if we push ourselves forward and try to do things we are not gifted to do, they will probably flop, and a whole bunch of people will be anything but blessed by our effort? It is important that we discover our natural and spiritual talents, and seek to develop them under the supervision of the Holy Spirit and wise leaders.

A few interesting verses are found in Exodus, chapters thirty-five and thirty-six. They address the people who were gifted for certain aspects of building and furnishing the Tabernacle in the wilderness. The principles used then apply to the building of the Church today. Where they built something physical, we build something spiritual.

All who are gifted artisans among you shall come and make all that the Lord has commanded.

Exodus 35:10

Note that the call is to the "gifted" artisans, not just anyone who has an ambition to do something for God.

And all the women whose heart stirred with a skill spun goats' hair.

Exodus 35:26, NAS

The spinning of goats' hair may not be a glamorous-sounding occupation, but, believe me, if God has gifted you to spin goats' hair, and it is needed for the building up of His sanctuary, it is as important as any job in the Church! The most important gift in the Church is the one that is needed at the moment. And notice the phrase, "whose hearts stirred with a skill." This is the key to your gifting and calling. Your heart may stir at the prospect of doing many things for God, but does it stir with a skill? Has God placed the raw ingredients of a particular talent within you? If not, leave it alone.

Two more verses worth noting are found in chapter thirty-six:

Now Bezalel and Oholiab, and every skillful person in whom the Lord has put a skill and understanding to know how to perform all the work in the construction of the sanctuary, shall perform in accordance with

all that the Lord has commanded. Then Moses called Bezalel and Oholiab and every skillful person in who the Lord had put skill, everyone whose heart stirred him, to come to the work and perform it.
Exodus 36:1-2, NAS

If God has placed a skill within you, there should be a better than ordinary ability to grasp and apply the knowledge needed to move ahead in the performance of that skill. If one hasn't an inborn ability to learn and develop a particular talent, it is likely that he should leave it alone. Let me give you a simple example:

I watch kids who want to be great guitar players; usually because of the recognition they think it will bring them. If the raw ingredients are there, within a few short months they will be able to do things an ungifted person would take years to do if they ever were able to do them at all. If the skill is not present, then no matter how hard they try, or how long they practice, they will not be able to produce something that blesses people. People need to be honest with themselves concerning the talents that may or may not be within them.

My spiritual brother, Billy Grant, is considered to be one of the best brick, block and rock masons anywhere in western Virginia. The knowledge, skill and energy with which he plies his trade are boundless and undeniable, even though he is no longer a young man. Laying up a block, rock or brick wall comes both easily and naturally to him. As a young man, when first learning his trade, he discovered that he had an aptitude for it. When methods were taught to him by his father and uncles, his natural skill became apparent, and he easily grasped and applied all that they taught him. The inner skill was present within Billy all along, it only needed to be developed. As a result, Billy's skill has been much in demand for many years, and he has never had to manipulate or coerce people into hiring him. A man's gift makes room for him, and brings him before great men (Proverbs 18:16). When a true skill is present inside you, and your heart stirs you to offer it to the work of the Lord, people will recognize and be drawn to it in your life.

Therefore, brethren, get in touch with what makes you tick. Beware of selfish ambition, and ask the Lord exactly what He wants you to do. If He asks you to do something, it is because He knows He has already placed the skill within you; all you need to do is develop it under the supervision of men and women who have been doing it longer than you have.

5. These were the other men God gave to assist Ezra in rebuilding Israel's spiritual condition, (8:16):

230

Eliezer – "God his help."
Ariel – "the lion of God."
Shemaiah – "whom Jehovah heard."
Elnathan – "whom God has given."
Jarib – "an adversary." (Hopefully to Ezra's enemies.)
Nathan – "given."
Zechariah – "Yahweh has remembered."
Meshullam – "befriended."
Joiarib – "whom Jehovah defends."
Iddo – "timely."

There were also the influential "heads of their clans" who were involved with Ezra (8:1-14). Ponder the meanings of their names and imagine how such men would benefit any team of kingdom builders:

Gershom – "expulsion," or "driven away."
Daniel – "God is my judge."
Hattush – "assembled."
Zechariah – "Jehovah is renowned."
Eliehoenai – "toward Jehovah are my eyes."
Ben-Jahaziel – "beheld by God."
Ebed – "servant."
Jeshaiah – "deliverance of Jehovah."
Zebadiah – "gift of Jehovah."
Obadiah – "servant of the Lord."
Ben-Josiphiah – "Jehovah will increase or add."
Johanan – "whom Jehovah graciously bestows."
Eliphelet – "God is his deliverance."
Jeiel – "snatched away by God," or "El takes away."
*Shemaiah – "whom Jehovah heard."
*Uthai – "Yahweh is my pride."
*Zabbud – "gift," or "given." (See Ezra 8:1-14.)

6. Sun Tzu (edited by James Clavell); *The Art of War;* Bantam Doubleday Dell Publishing Group, Inc.; New York, N.Y.; 1983; p. 54

7. Nehemiah's team of people accomplished a tremendous work as God's hand was upon their leader. The meanings of their names give us an idea of the various strengths and talents they brought to the team. There was:

Nehemiah — "comforted by Jehovah."
Eliashib the high priest — "whom God will restore."

Zaccur — "mindful."

Meremoth — "exaltations, heights."

Meshullam — "befriended."

Jehoiada — "Jehovah known."

Melatiah — "Jehovah has delivered."

Jadon — "judge."

Uzziel — "strength of God."

Rephaiah — "Jehovah heals."

Jedaiah — "invoker of Jehovah."

Hattush — "assembled."

Malchijah — "Jehovah's king."

Hashub — "intelligent."

Shallum — "retribution."

Hanun — "graciously given."

Rehum — "merciful."

Hashabiah — "regarded by Jehovah."

Bavai or Binnui — "built."

Ezer — "treasure."

Baruch — "blessed."

Benjamin — "son of my right hand."

Azariah — "whom Jehovah helps."

Palal — "God judges."

Pedaiah — "redemption of the Lord."

Zadok — "righteous."

Shemaiah — "whom Jehovah heard."

8. In coming years, the spirit of Jezebel will attempt to wield great influence on worldly political systems. Many Ahab and Herod-type leaders will find it politically advantageous to yield to this threatening spirit, even though they have no idea that is what they are doing. But another influence will also arise, one that will frustrate the spirit of Jezebel. With great conviction and brass, a new generation of Hazaels, Jehus, and Elishas will come forth (see 1 Kings 19:15-17), and Jezebel's empire, which will find its own culmination in the whore of Revelation, will crash and burn. (See Revelation 17 and 18.)

It is interesting to note that the Syrian king, Hazael, was used by God to help bring an end to Jezebel's wicked influence. Once this evil man gained authority over Syria (2 Kings 8:12-15—at a time of relative peace between his nation and Israel), he turned and sent his armies to fight the Jews, "conquering them in all the territory of Israel" (2 Kings 10:32). By this he damaged Jezebel, for she had seized control of Israel through her weak husband, Ahab.

As an Old Testament figure, Hazael foreshadows the "man of peace" (the Antichrist), who in the Tribulation period, will turn, not only on Israel, but also on the Harlot. The Antichrist will lead a confederation of nations to "hate the harlot, make her desolate and naked, eat her flesh and burn her with fire" (17:16). And so we see that feminism, a harlot religious system, and corrupt financial and political systems—all in bed together—will eventually be destroyed by the interesting interplay of three unique entities: a praying, Elisha-like remnant, a violent Jehu-like political leadership (2 Kings 9:1-8, 30-33; 10:31-36—favorable to Judeo-Christian culture, but not godly), and finally, a Hazael-like world ruler (the Antichrist), who will seek to destroy the Harlot, as well as anyone who resists his rule. This Hazael-like destroyer of the Jezebel spirit may also typify the huge Islamic fundamentalist movement that hates the same thing about western nations that the remnant Church hates about western nations. If the leaders of Islamic Jihad had their way in the west, some of the first people to be exterminated would be the radical feminists and homosexuals. If the feminists and homosexuals think the Church is bigoted, wait till they have to face the Muslims after the Church is taken out. This horrendous scene may well be described in Revelation's seventeenth and eighteenth chapters!

But let us now look more closely at the spirit of Jezebel. This evil spiritual queen, and her radical feminist exertions in any age, are truly despised and hated in all nations! Except for those deceived by her lies or frightened by her wrath, the world at large resists her. Sadly, in some western nations, large numbers of people are presently captivated by this antichristian spiritual power. Even so, the curse imposed on rebellious women in Genesis 3:16, will remain intact until Messiah returns in power and glory. Therefore, until then, women who attempt to assert their godless agendas for society will continue to meet formidable and undying resistance. The Elijah's, Jehu's and Hazael's of the world, although vastly different from each other in nearly every other category, will continue to be the feminists greatest adversaries. In the end, Jezebel-type women will only heap more trouble on themselves. The curse on women will actually be strengthened by their abhorrent behavior. When they screech and growl their protests in speeches and press conferences, they will only intensify the disgust felt by many who hear them. When they point their fingers, shake their fists, and declare their intentions for society, it will only stir the ire of their enemies. But right on the other hand, women who keep their proper bearing as God-fearing members of society, will attract and retain the honor due them as sisters, wives and mothers (1 Peter 3:1-4; 1 Timothy 2:9-15; 5:3-16). Only in Christ is the curse lifted from women, and as believers' seeking to lead exemplary lives in the nature of their Lord, God Himself will watch over them, looking favorably on them because of their commitment to live by His Word. He knows and rejoices that their day of ultimate freedom and glory is coming. When rewards are handed out at the Judgment Seat of Christ, I believe the overwhelming majority of recipients will be women who loved and served the Lord with pure and devoted hearts. Such women invoke the love and respect rightfully due to women. Indeed, in all but a few societies worldwide, women are loved and respected *when* they lead respectable lives. The other kinds of women—those who attempt to wrest power by demanding it, actually push it away. Only men possessed by a Herod spirit care what these biddies have to say.

One more note about Herod Antipas. He also sanctioned John's murder because "of those who sat with him" (Matthew 14:9). He was so worried about what his friends thought of him, that he was willing to do anything to keep their approval. These friends might have been comprised of representatives of the special interest groups of his day; those who promised their support *if* he would grant them special favors. Because he rubbed elbows with these people, he somehow felt obligated to feed their desires. Instead of standing with his own conscience, he allowed his desire for their approval to guide him in his final decision concerning John. The old classic movie, *Mr. Smith Goes to Washington,* could not have been written about Ahab, Herod, or many of today's political leaders.

9. In Biblical times the loins were considered to be the seat of a person's strength and power; his true center of gravity (Deuteronomy 33:11; Job 40:16; Proverbs 31:17; Nahum 2:1). For a successful run to Jezreel, Elijah would have to muster his strength and start moving. A *kairos* moment was before him, and to approach it with anything but energy and passion would have displeased the Lord. As the prophet employed his own strength to begin the dash, he soon discovered a supernatural strength coming alongside to anoint him for a successful race.

Paul taught that the Holy Spirit "helps in our weaknesses" (Romans 8:26.)The word translated *helps* in this verse means "to take hold with one." This is precisely what the Holy Spirit does for us as we step out to obey God. The task before us may require much more strength and wisdom we have within ourselves, but as we step into it, God's power rushes to our side to add His strength and wisdom to ours. Thus, He takes hold with us against the negative forces of the situation.

What else did Elijah need to gird up besides his strength? I believe he had to gird up his feelings! In those days the loins were also considered to be the center of one's emotions. Elijah had just come through an emotional showdown with 850 Old Testament antichrists, and through a stunning display of faith, he had moved the Hand that controls the lightning! And if that weren't enough, he had personally overseen the execution of all 850 false prophets, watching as the brook Kishon flowed red with their idolatrous blood. Elijah's emotions must have been soaring! Great indignation mixed with deep sorrow surely grappled within his loins, and he was probably exhausted. When the time came for a dash to Jezreel, he had to "pull it together." By his patience he had to possess his soul (his mind, will and emotions), rather than let his soul control his responses (Luke 21:19).

How about you, beloved? Are you facing a mammoth contest at the moment? Your natural tendency may be to stick your head in the sand and hope it will all go away, but that is not the response for which God is looking. Ignoring a problem will not make it disappear. Closing your eyes to it will only exacerbate matters. The Lord would say to you:

Gird up now your loins like a man! (Job 38:3). Tap into My power by stirring up your own, says the Lord. For as you step forth, you will discover My strength coming alongside to give you victory in the contest. As Eleazar found out, in the heat of battle, that his hand was fused supernaturally to his sword, so you must find that My strength will anoint you to wrest decisive victories from the jaws of defeat! And as Peter girded his loins and stepped from the unsure safety of the storm-tossed boat before experiencing My power, so you must muster your courage to step into the exploits I've called you to, says the Lord. For I ask you, "What is that in your hand?" Employ it in faith and watch as the irresistible strength of My anointing comes to bear on your situation..

In his first letter, Peter exhorts, "Therefore gird up the loins of your mind, be sober, and rest your hope fully upon the grace that is to be brought to you at the revelation of Jesus Christ" (1 Peter 1:13). The human mind is the battleground where opposing forces either win or lose. If we can defeat Satan in the mind, we can defeat him anywhere. If he can defeat us in the mind, he can defeat our every purpose. This is the rule of law for the terrorist. If he can get inside the minds of his enemies, he will defeat them. Their fear of him will bring inner defeat, which will eventually bring outward defeat. That is why the Psalmist prayed, "Lord, deliver me from fear of the enemy" (Psalm 64:1). It is not the enemy we need to address initially, but rather, fear of the enemy. We should not take counsel of our fears. But how? By taking counsel of our God! If we can eliminate fear by being ensconced in an absolute trust of God, enormous spiritual forces will go to work in our behalf, and eliminate the enemy. Beloved, if we can but maintain the high ground of the mind when facing an enemy, we will secure victory and still be standing when the smoke has cleared away.

The believer maintains the high ground when he holds on to God's perspective amidst severe trials. The believer maintains the high ground when he keeps looking at unseen eternal realities instead of temporal contradictions. He maintains the high ground when he keeps God's Word before his eyes, in the midst of his heart, and on a grateful tongue. He maintains the high ground when he holds himself calm in the days of adversity.

In Ephesians, Paul lists the armor a Christian should wear while living and operating on this battlefield called earth. Of all the pieces of armor listed, the loinbelt of truth is the most essential. The analogy of the armor is taken from the equipment a Roman legionary donned in Paul's day. When going into battle, everything a Roman soldier wore would be directly or indirectly connected to his belt. Therefore, in a sense, the loinbelt held it all together. His armor would simply fall apart if he did not have his loinbelt fastened securely.

As Christians everything we have and everything we do must be connected to the belt of truth. Our loins (strength and emotions) must be girt about with the Word of God. God never wants us to react emotionally to pressure, but respond calmly in faith. Without securing our every thought, word and deed to the written Word of God, we will be guilty of praying unscriptural prayers, speaking unscriptural words, and carrying out unscriptural deeds that displease and grieve the Holy Spirit. Not only that, but we will also make ourselves more vulnerable to Satan's attack as our armor falls apart.

Isaiah prophesied that righteousness would be the belt of Jesus' loins, and faithfulness the belt of His waist (Isaiah 11:5). Jesus accomplished His earthly mission exactly as planned because His loins were girded with truth, righteousness and faithfulness. The righteous conduct befitting a man of God, as well as the faithfulness he exhibits toward his many responsibilities, enables him to experience the Lord's mighty hand of power. The man who fails to gird up the loins of right conduct and faithfulness when the hand of God is coming upon him, will be unable to move into the victories God desires.

10. Dick Eastman, *Heights of Delight,* Ventura, CA: Regal Books, 2002, p. 52.

11. Edwin Way Teale; *Journey into Summer;* Dodd, Meade & Company; New York; 1960; p. 6.

12. James B. Hodgkin; *Home Life of Gen. R. E. Lee's Family;* Confederate Veteran 15; Sept. 1907; 399.

13. Colvar; *A Boy's Observations of Gen. Lee;* 265.

14. On the Mount of Transfiguration, the glory cloud overshadowed Peter and the Father spoke from Heaven concerning Jesus: "This is my beloved Son, in whom I am well pleased. Hear Him!" (Matthew 17:5). Nowhere in the Bible does it say we are to hear anyone else regarding the key issues of life and death. The words Jesus spoke are supreme! In fact, Paul said that God has appointed a day when He will judge the world <u>by that Man</u> He raised from the dead (Acts 17:31). Jesus, the resurrected Messiah, is at the end of the road for every man and woman! No one will escape a personal appearance before His majestic throne in glory. The word He has spoken will be the judge in the last day, and that will be a day of sentencing (John 12:48). Those who have received Jesus Christ as Lord and Savior will be rewarded, and those who have refused Him will be damned. And so, God's voice from Heaven said, "Hear Him! Let all others be silent and listen to what My Son has to say!"

And what did Jesus have to say? He said many powerful things, but one defining statement made in Jerusalem should settle our question forever. In John's gospel, the Lord is recorded as saying: "He who does not honor the Son does not honor the Father who sent Him" (5:23). Do you see the significance of this statement? Without honoring Jesus, a person cannot truly honor the Father. When the adherent to another religion seeks to honor God by honoring someone other than Jesus Christ, he misses the mark terribly and completely. How can Allah, the god of the Muslim, and the Heavenly Father, the God of the Christian, be one in the same if He is honored when Jesus is revered, but also when Mohammed is revered? The Christian's God is only honored when His people praise and worship Jesus. The Muslim's god is only honored when his people embrace and revere Mohammed and his teaching. On Judgment Day, whose word will judge the world? If the Father is honored when both Mohammed and Jesus are exalted, although they are at opposite ends of the spectrum in both nature and doctrine, then Jesus lied to us and the Father is schizophrenic! And we know that's not the case. According to Jesus, the Father receives honor and glory *only as* people exalt and give honor to Christ. That is why a Muslim and a Christian do not worship the same God. Most Muslims understand the difference. Christians in most of the world understand it too. Why can't American Christians realize it and stop trying to act like as though Islam is a religion to be embraced? It is nothing but a manifestation of the spirit of antichrist John said would be released in the last days (1 John 2:18). The prefix *anti* has two meanings in the Greek language: First, "in place of," and second, "against." These two meanings describe Islamic doctrine to the letter. Muslims believe Mohammed arrived on earth in the seventh century to replace Jesus Christ as the revelation of God to men. They teach that, although Jesus was a wonderful teacher/prophet in His day, He is no longer current but obsolete. This is the spirit of antichrist! The Muslim's message will not gather people to the kingdom Jesus came to initiate and set up. He said, "He who is not with Me is against me, and he who does not gather with Me scatters abroad" (Matthew 12:30).

Many years ago, I heard renowned Bible scholar and teacher, Derek Prince, identify the spirit of Islam as the number one force opposing Christianity on earth. I agreed with him then, and I agree with him now. The world at large must deal with this universal threat to mankind. This spirit is the epitome of fascism, more enormous and threatening than communism and humanism combined. Nothing but a powerful display of God's mighty hand will drag it from its seat of power in heavenly places. And this is beginning to happen.

One method God is using to convince Muslims of Christ's present day Lordship is the outpouring of signs, wonders and miracles. When He heals them of their dreaded diseases in third world environments where medical help is hard to come by, they are gripped by His love and care for them. He has also been appearing to thousands of them in open visions. Every week we hear more marvelous testimonies of Muslims who have been convinced of Christ's Lordship as they've seen Him walking the streets of their villages, or had Him come to them in a dream.

As wonderful as these stories are, other Muslims are beginning to experience God's hand in lethal ways. What happened to the two despicable sons of Saddam Hussein was a form of judgment, even though He used men to execute it. When David killed Goliath, he carried out God's judgment against a proud, evil and boastful man. God is not beyond using warriors today in like manner. The way Hussein's sons tortured and terrorized the people of Iraq was unheard of. I once saw a bootleg videotape of one of their infamous parties. On the film, a man was blindfolded and made to kneel on the floor before Hussein's wicked sons. While they looked on with joy, an executioner stepped forward with a hammer and screwdriver, and slowly drove the screwdriver into the kneeling man's head. This produced pleasure for the two boys. Only God knows what other forms of torture pleased these two monsters? Evil like this must be stopped, and will be stopped sooner or later! Paul said, "Some men's sins are clearly evident (and dealt with), preceding

238

them to judgment, but those of some men follow later" (1 Timothy 5:24). The clear evidence of wickedness seen in the wanton slaughter carried out by Islamic terrorists in the days ahead will call for the hard hand of God's judgment to fall. When God calls their number, and they are eradicated in the days to come, God will be doing the world a great service!

15. *Webster's New World College Dictionary;* MacMillan General Reference, New York, NY; 199; p. 575.

16. Zechariah 12:2

17. Zechariah 12:3

OTHER CHIP HILL BOOKS

FRONT LINE WARFARE: is an instruction book for believers who find themselves in the trenches for God's Kingdom. Many uplifting and practical nuggets of truth designed to help you succeed in life's battles are found within the pages of this end-times manual. 230 pages of straightforward, no-nonsense teaching for the serious disciple of Christ.

$9.00

INVISIBLE WILDERNESS: The Appalachian Mountains in 1755 were a harsh and dangerous wilderness. A pioneer named Andrew Woodlief was called of God to invade the savagery of this wilderness with the gospel of Jesus Christ. It didn't matter that both a natural and a spiritual frontier opposed him; he was determined to accomplish his mission. Against all odds, Andrew battles the ignorance of sin-bound men, as well as the treachery of a well-developed demonic army - and wins! "*Invisible Wilderness*" will show you the gospel as it should be presented - in power and with great resolve. The name of Andrew Woodlief will be etched forever in your heart as an example of devotion and spiritual militancy, when you encounter the unseen forces of darkness that are bound to arise in these days. **$8.00**

MANTLES OF ANOINTING: explores many of the special anointings God has for His people - those divine enablements the Church needs in order to be effective and fruitful in this fallen world. Some of the special anointings covered in this volume are the mantles of healing, spiritual warfare, the scribe and many more. This little book is a best seller, and promises to encourage your effectiveness in the ministry. 63 pages.

$7.00

DYNAMICS OF REVIVAL: A Christian revival of immense proportions is currently breaking onto the world. Many have not comprehended what is involved in such mighty outpourings of the Spirit, and so they fear, dismiss or fight it outright. The time has come for people everywhere to understand and flow into all God is doing as He manifests His glory amidst those of us "upon whom the ends of the ages has come." *Dynamics* is for those seeking understanding and historical validation of God's present move. It was written to encourage your own personal revival, as well as to stir and renew your mission in this great flood of God's glory. **$10.00**

WARRIORS BY BLOOD: A Revival of immense proportions is engulfing the nations of the earth. We are facing an age where contagious evangelism is made sim-ple by sovereign outbreaks of the Spirit of God. Many of us who have longed to see this harvest of souls still do not fully understand the levels of spiritual warfare into which we are about to be thrust. We still do not understand who Jehovah-Sabaoth (the Lord of Armies) has appointed us to be. Warriors by Blood was written to both remove the veil of traditional thought which dulls our hearts, as well as to revive the sacred passion imprinted in our blood. Read it and rise up! **$9.00**

For details about purchasing any or many of these books, please send a check, made payable to:

"Word of Faith Bookstore"
P. O. Box 276
Monterey, VA 24465

and include $2.50 for Shipping & Handling Charges.

Sorry, but we are not set up to accept credit cards at this time. Any questions, please call (540) 468-2592, email us at *highrsvt@cfw.com,* or visit *www.chiphill.org.*